THE OGRI COLLECTION

by Paul Sample ©

**BUMPER SELECTION OF OGRI CARTOONS!
VOLUMES 1-3 COMBINED,
PLUS EXTRA MATERIAL**

GRRR!

Haynes Publishing

Most of the material in this book first appeared in *Ogri Volume 1*, published in 1981 by Talisman Books, *Ogri Volume 2*, published in 1983 by Ogri Products, and *Ogri Volume 3*, published in 1992 by Ogri Marketing Ltd. *The Ogri Collection* was first published by Haynes Publishing in December 1998, with additions.

A catalogue record for this book is available from the British Library

ISBN 1 85960 616 4

Library of Congress catalog card no 98-73714

Haynes North America Inc., 861 Lawrence Drive, Newbury Park, California 91320, USA.

Published by Haynes Publishing, Sparkford, Nr Yeovil, Somerset BA22 7JJ, UK.
Tel: 01963 440635 Fax: 01963 440001
Int.tel: +44 1963 440635 Int.fax: +44 1963 440001
E-mail: sales@haynes-manuals.co.uk
Web site: http://www.haynes.com

OGRI MERCHANDISE
A full range of Ogri merchandise is available from Ogri Ltd, 5 Civic Green Workshops, Whitchurch, Shropshire, SY13 1LA (Tel. 01948 667732). Free catalogue on request.

Printed and bound in Great Britain by J. H. Haynes & Co. Ltd., Sparkford

INTRODUCTION

I'LL SKIP THIS BIT...!

When Paul Sample was a student, when they still had trolley buses in Bradford and a pint of bitter cost less than 10p, and passion-killing tights hadn't been invented, he bought himself a motorcycle. From that event which changed his life, the idea of a cartoon based on the trials, tribulations, frustrations and joys of owning and riding a motorcycle entered his head, and subsequently appeared as doodles and sketches in the notebooks he kept throughout his college years studying at the Central School of Art in London. Some of those sketches are reproduced here.

That was in 1968. Over the following few years the character metamorphosed from a piss-take on the Thor and Superman type hero battling against amorphic villains and spurious injustices to a somewhat more down-to-earth hero. He drank Newkie Brown (because the Truman's beer in London was foul), built impossibly fast and powerful special bikes to ride (because bikes were horribly slow dogs), and could pull a girl by his silent charisma alone (dream on laddie). Everything, well nearly everything, worked for Ogri. He was the biker every biker wanted to be. No, that's not true. He was the biker Paul Sample wanted to be. The reality of the story is of course that he and all novice bikers are in fact 'Malcolms' - vulnerable, innocent of the workings of a motorcycle, for ever making mistakes, lacking confidence in the presence of females, and generally being a complete dork with no social graces to speak of.

Many of the strips are based on true stories, often on the personal experiences of the author. HE was the idiot who wrapped a sidecar up the arse of a stationary double decker bus. HE was the one who put an aluminium cylinder head in caustic soda to clean off the carbon. HE was the one who...

Anyway, enough to say that he used all these experiences to develop the characters of Ogri and Malcolm in the strip cartoons.

The first strip was published in Bike magazine in 1972. From that point it progressed into a vehicle for telling stories and making comments on the world, not just of biking, but of all the prejudices, silly posturing and great mess and daftness that goes on around the social and domestic sea of life that everybody paddles about in.

The strip isn't just for bikers, but for everyone who can bear and enjoy to see a bit of fun poked at themselves, their neighbours, their family, and even their pets. And talking of pets, Ogri's dog Kickstart is based on a real dog. Kickstart thinks he is many times reincarnated - he was a philosopher and a cynic, a war hero and a casanova, a world-beating motorcycle racer, a chariot racer, a card sharp, and a guru. He believes he has been all these and is now, by some horrible quirk of fate, trapped in the body of a dog, a short life he expects to endure and enjoy. But we all know he's just a dog.

Paul Sample tells me that he is embarrassed at how gauche some of the early strips are, but he was young and not so cynical then.

Enjoy!

Professor Heime B. Barking Madstein, Kt. T.T., D.D.T., B.F. (& bar), L.I.A.R. (hon), University Institution of Congenital Insecurity, Batley 1998

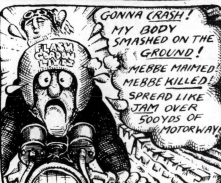

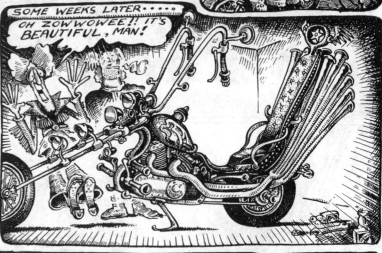

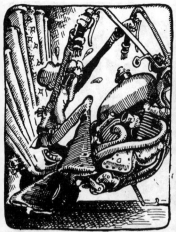

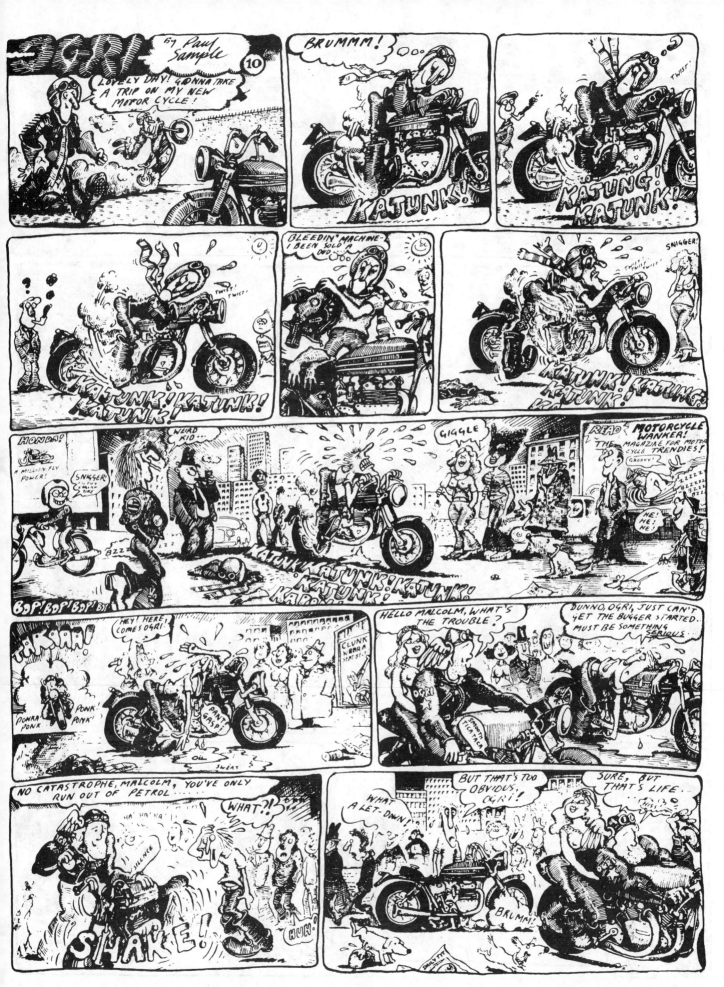

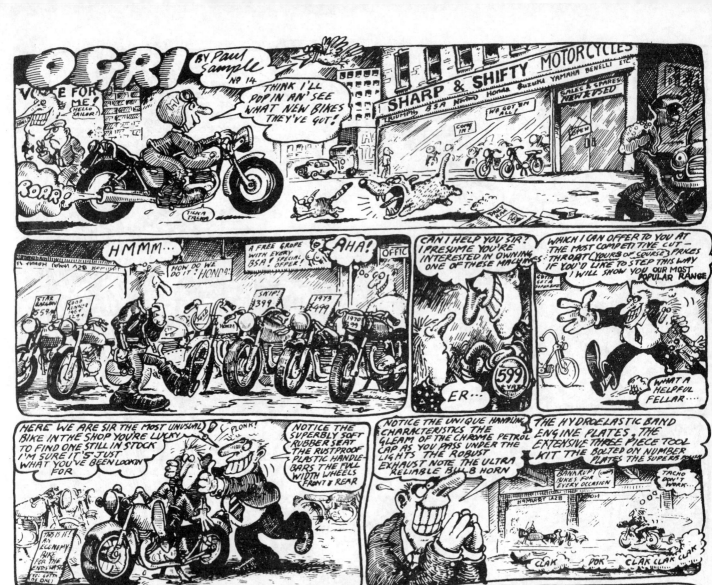

29

34

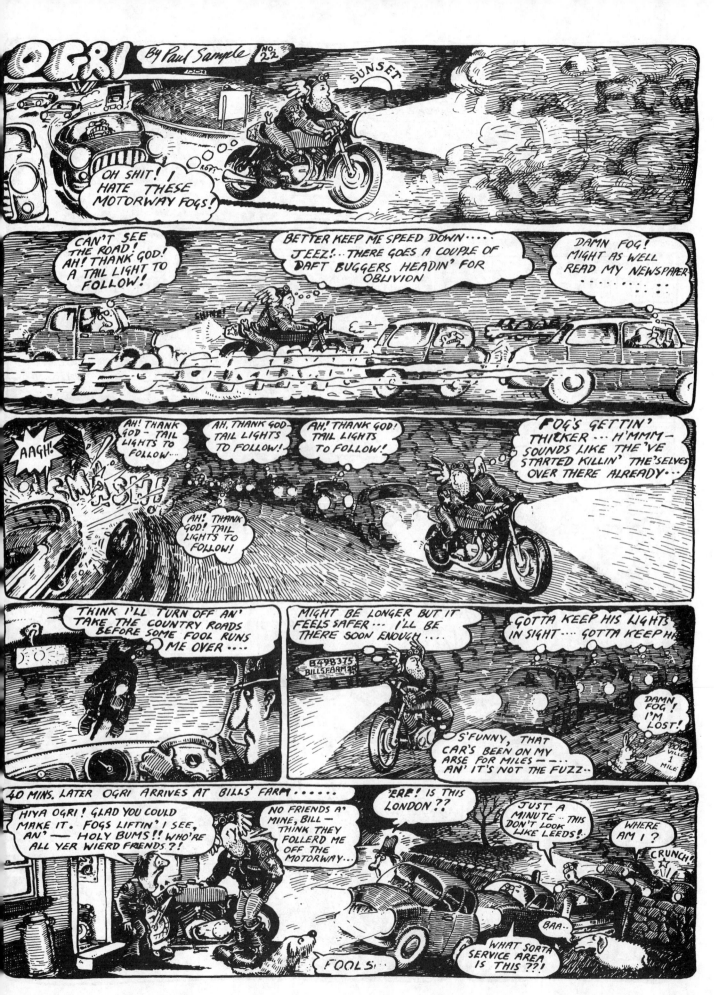

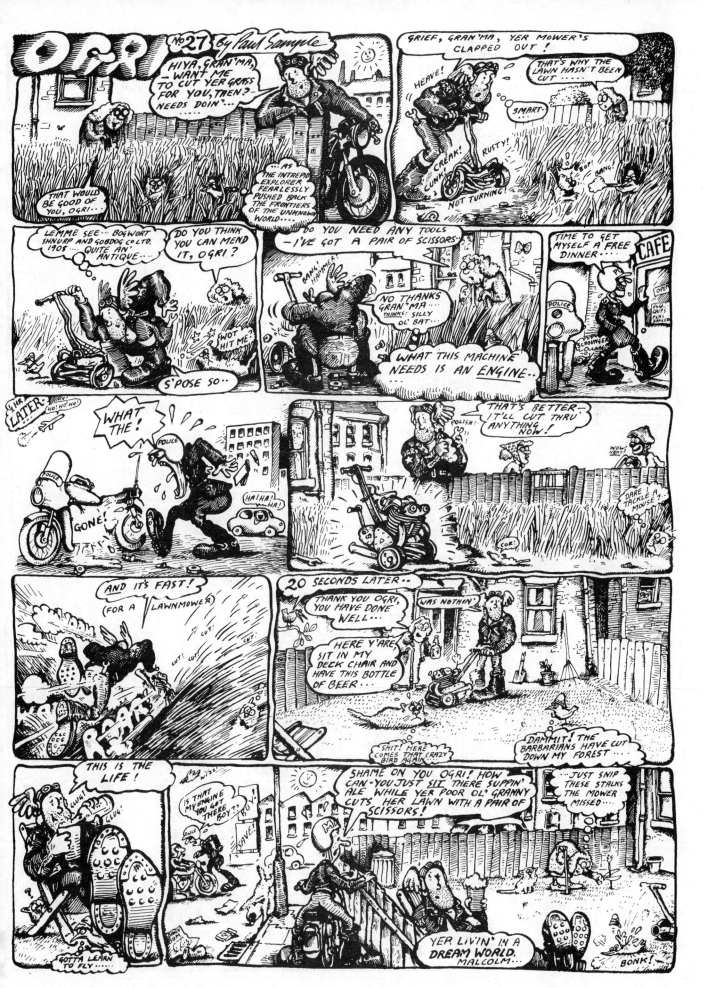

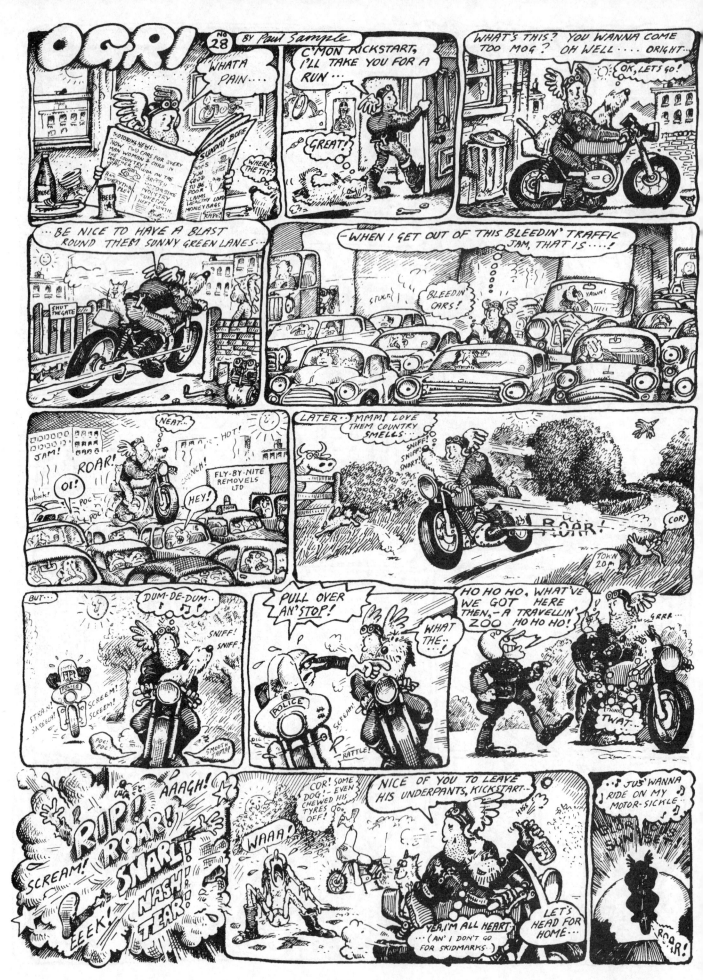

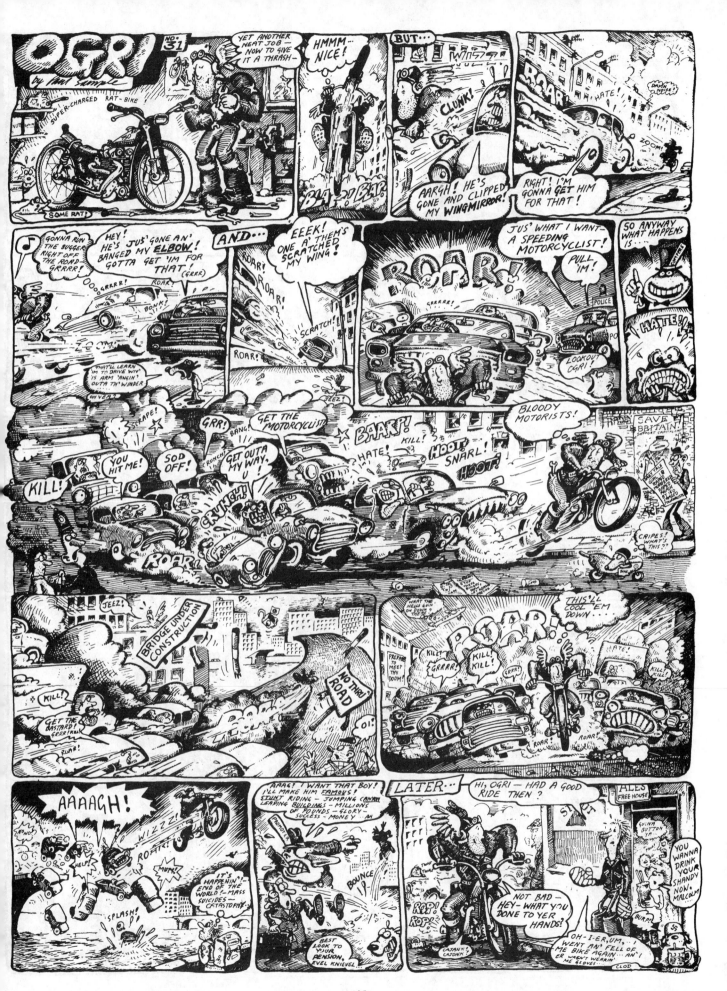

45

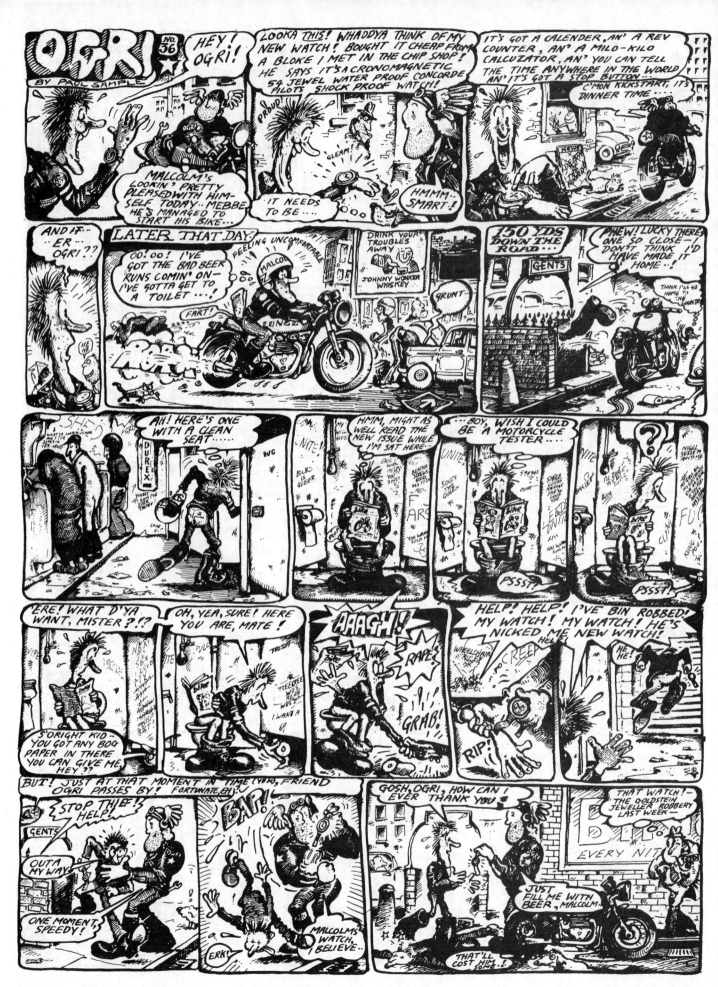

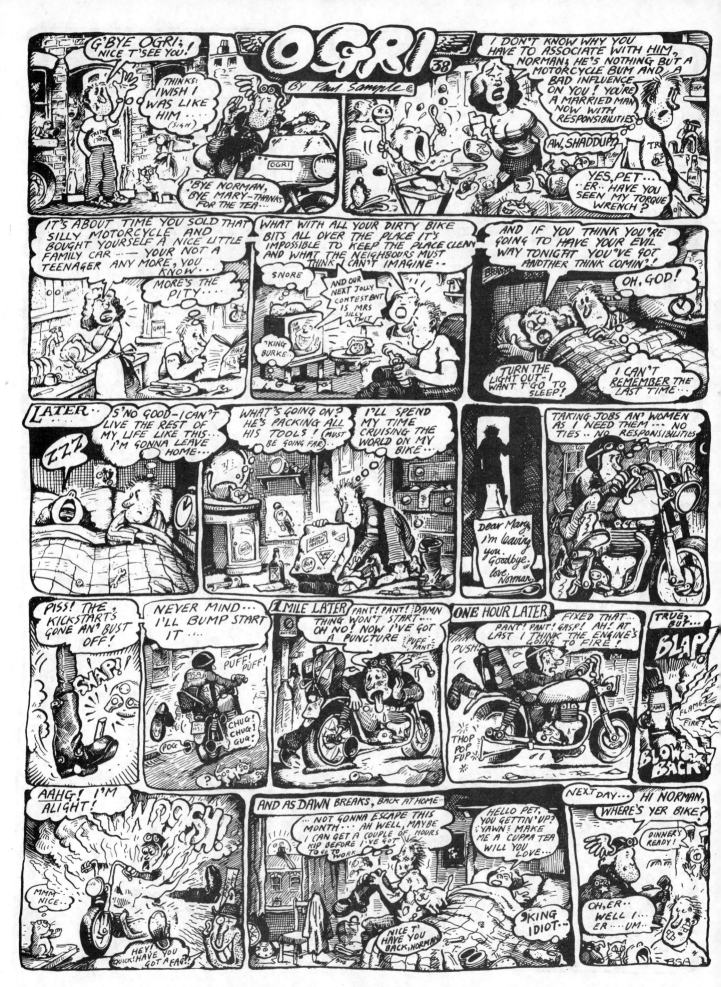

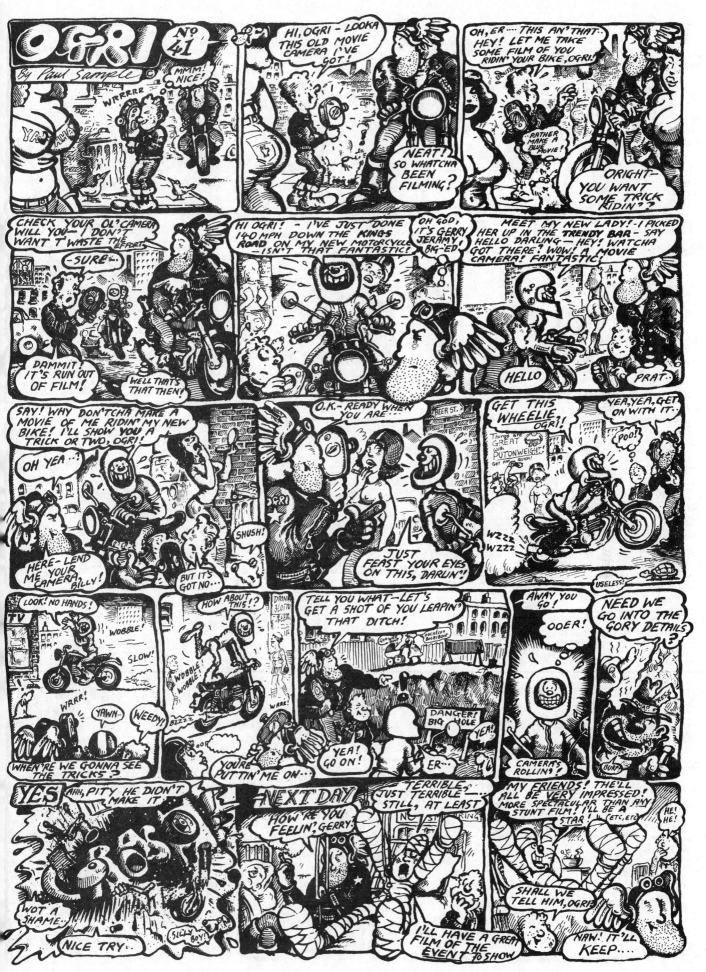

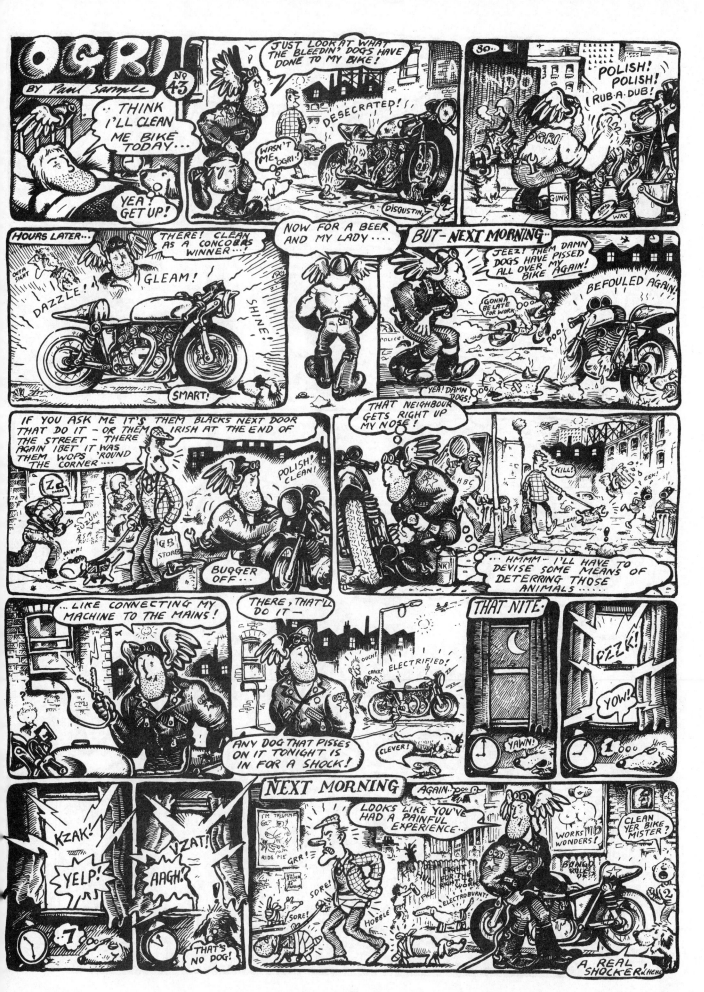

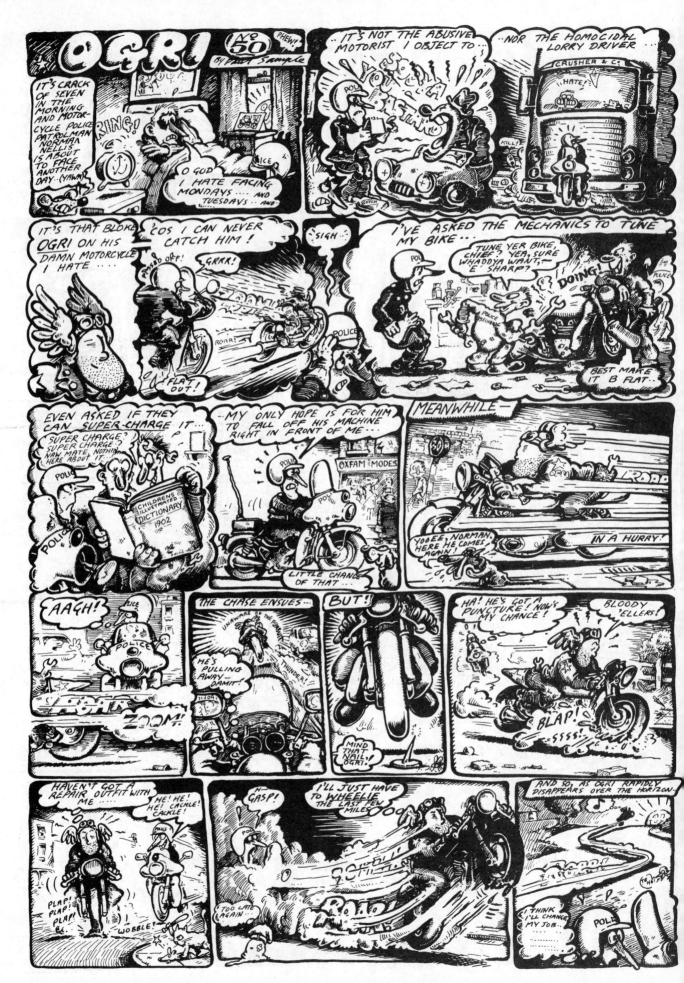

64

65

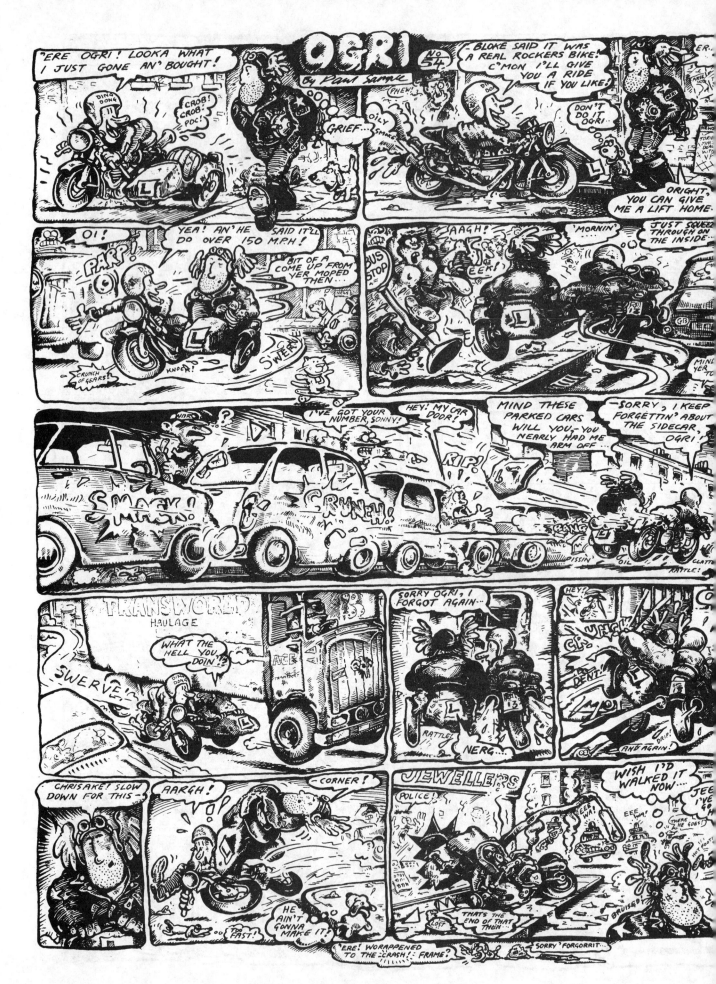

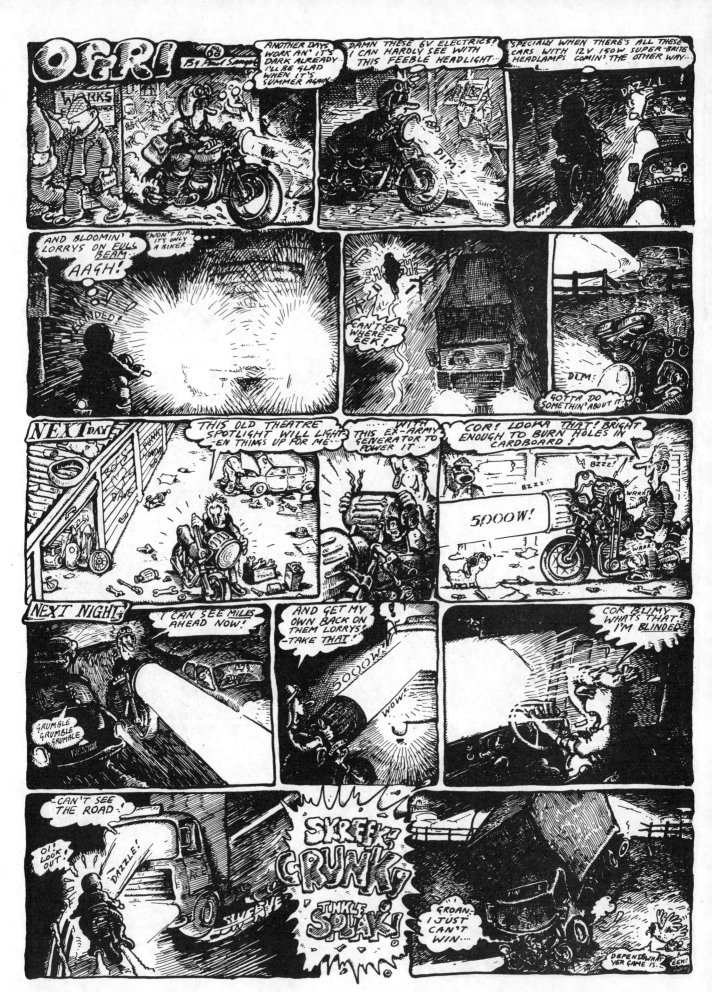

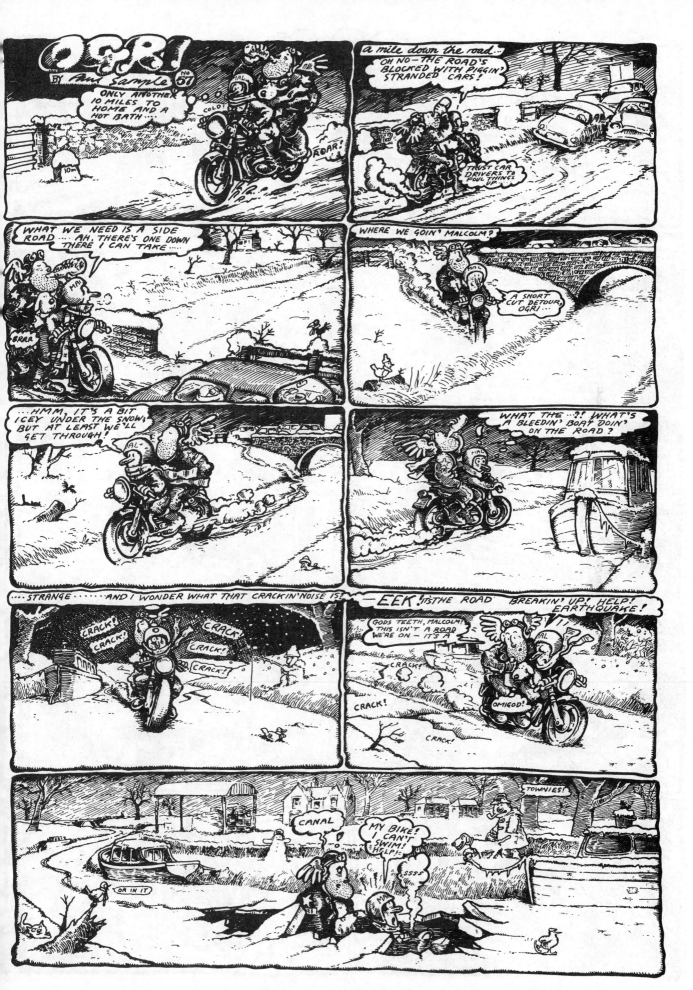

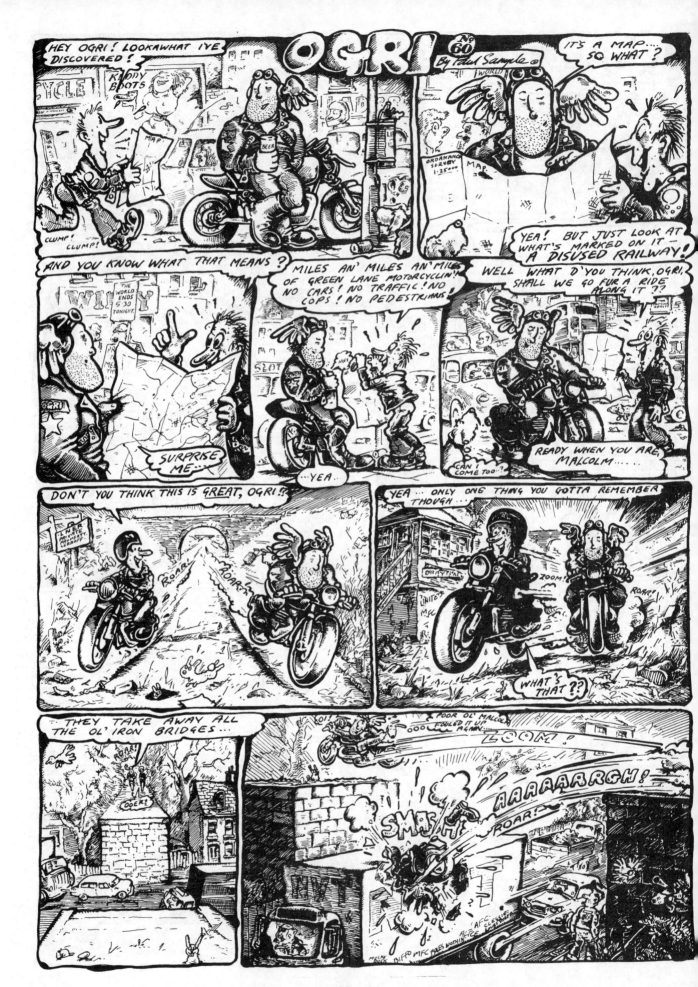

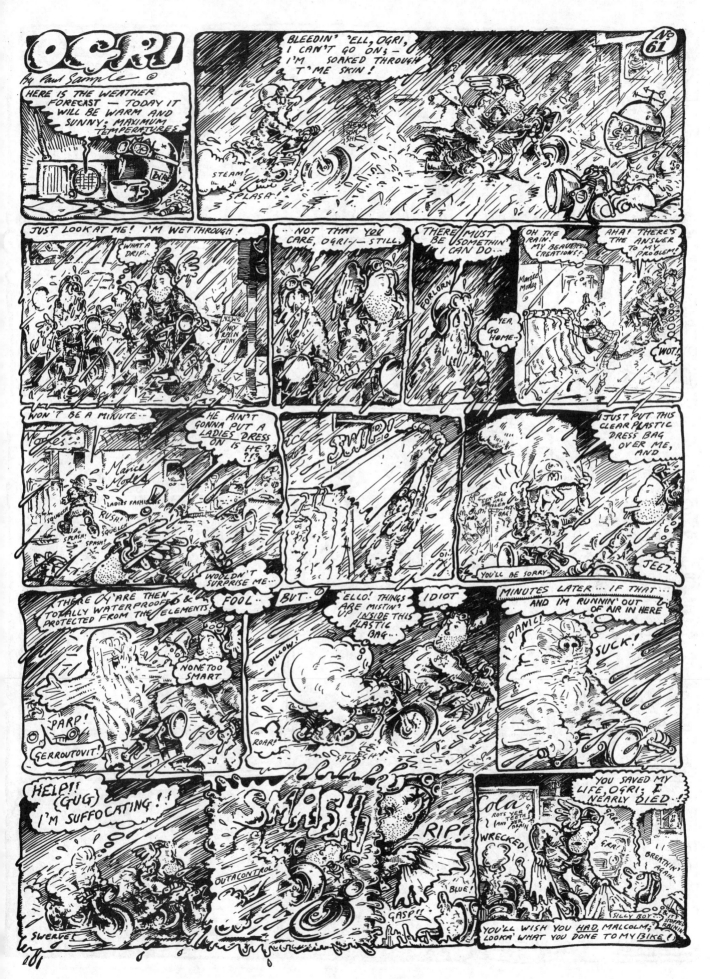

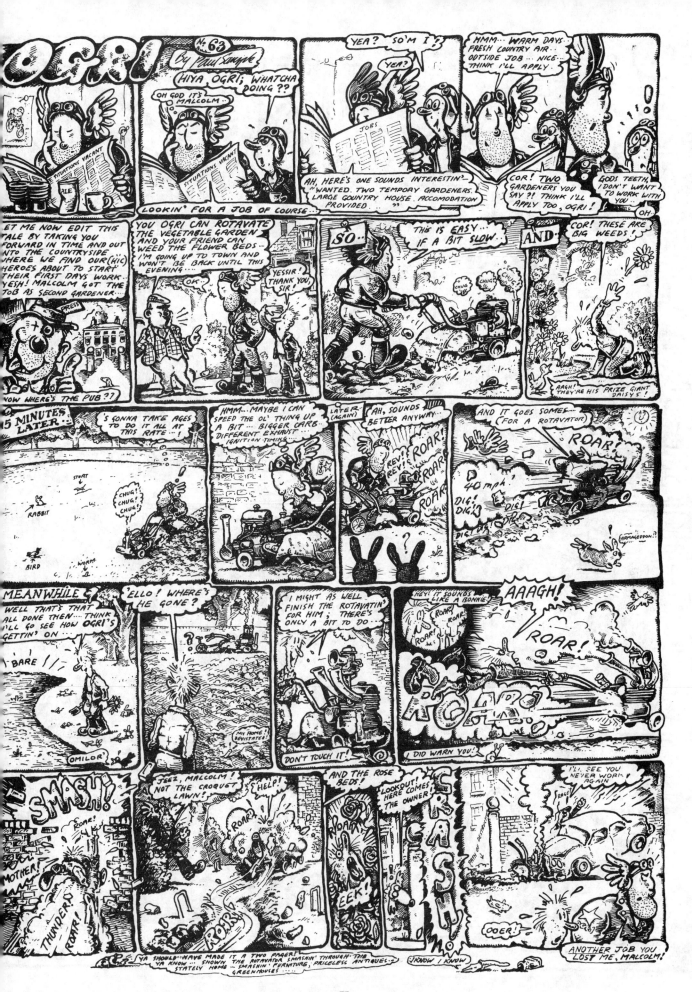

78

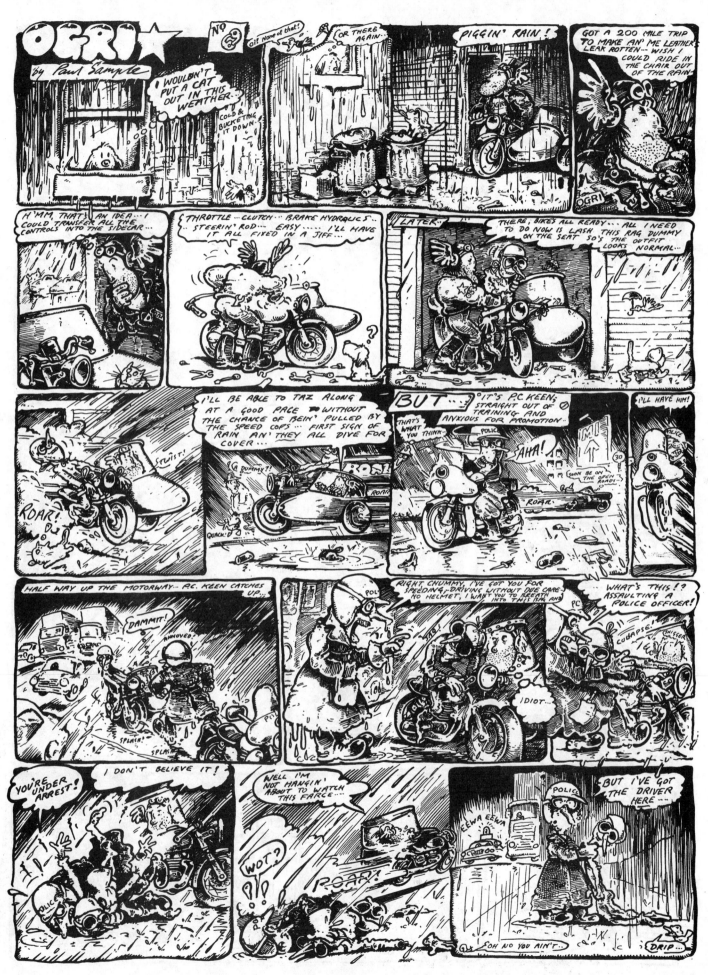

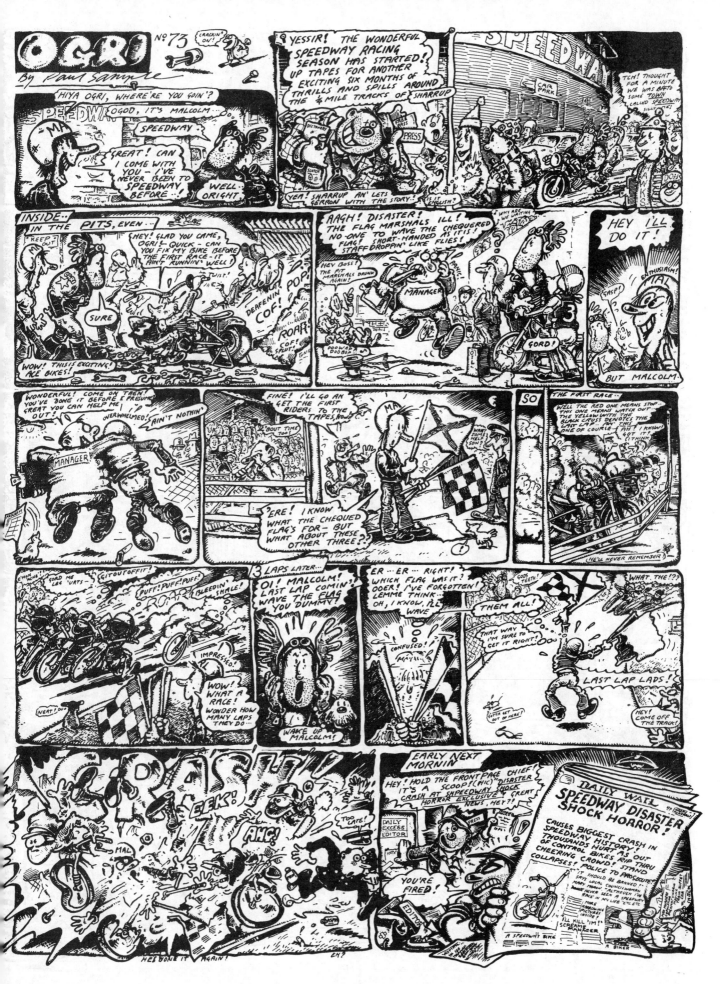

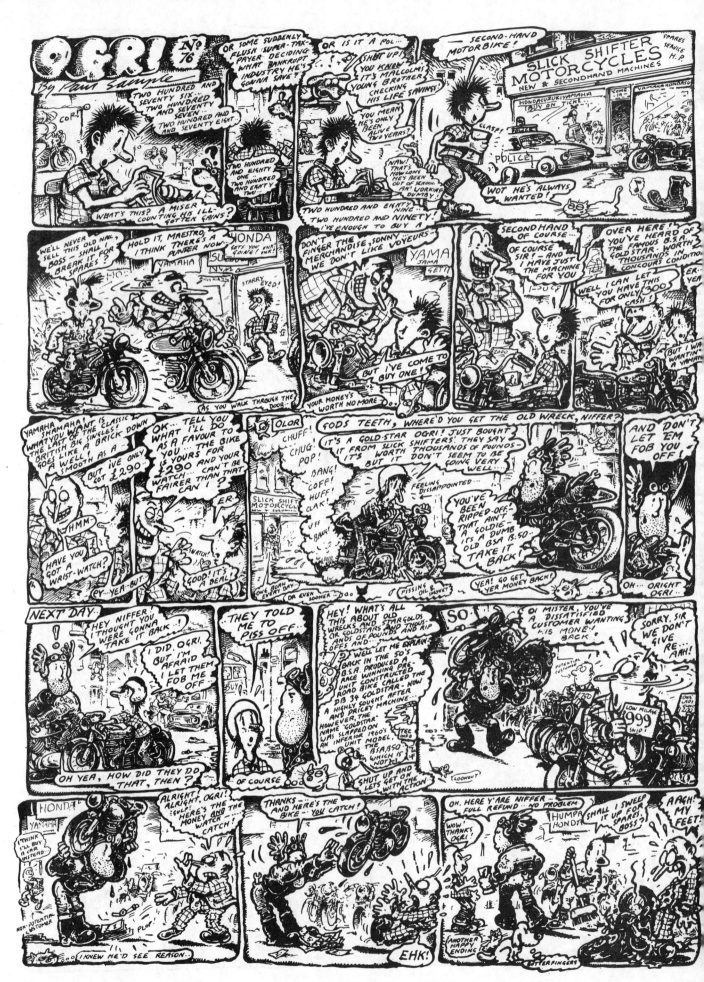

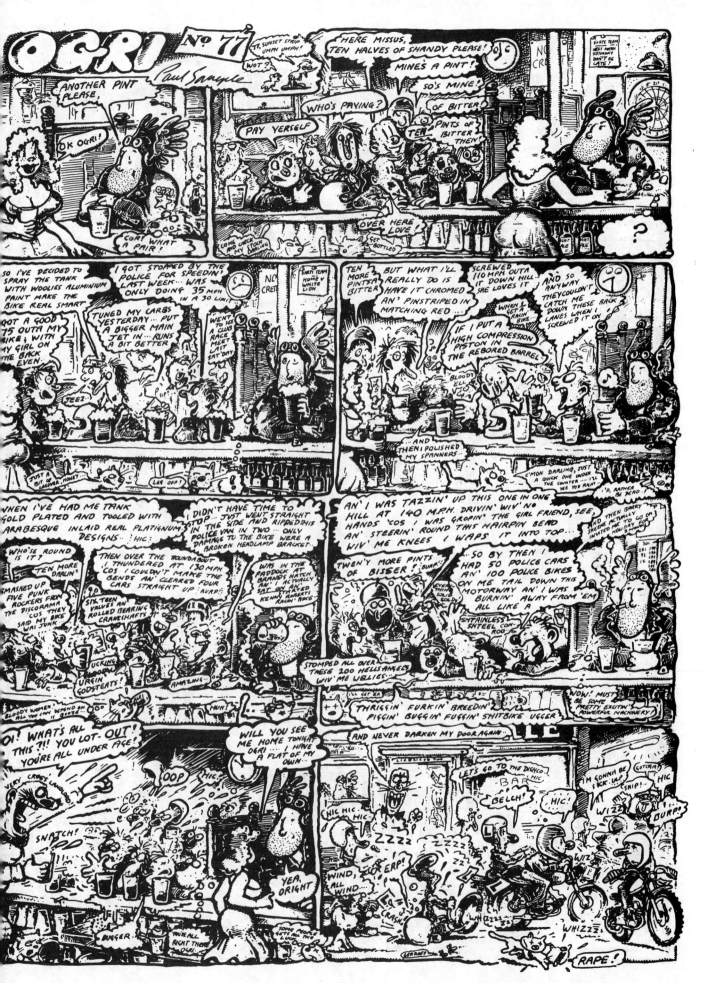

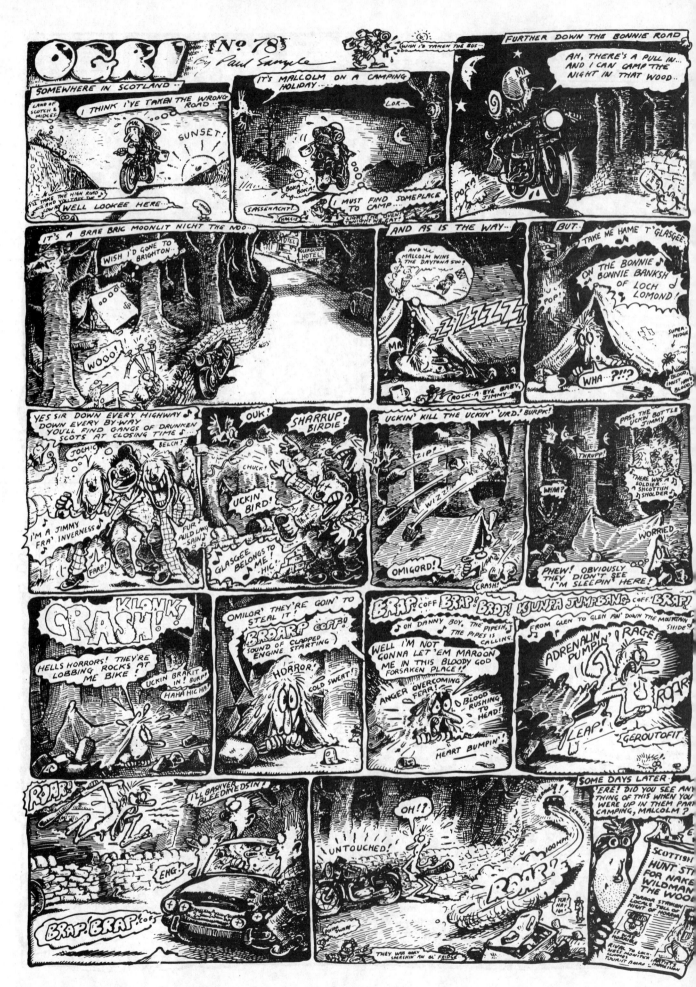

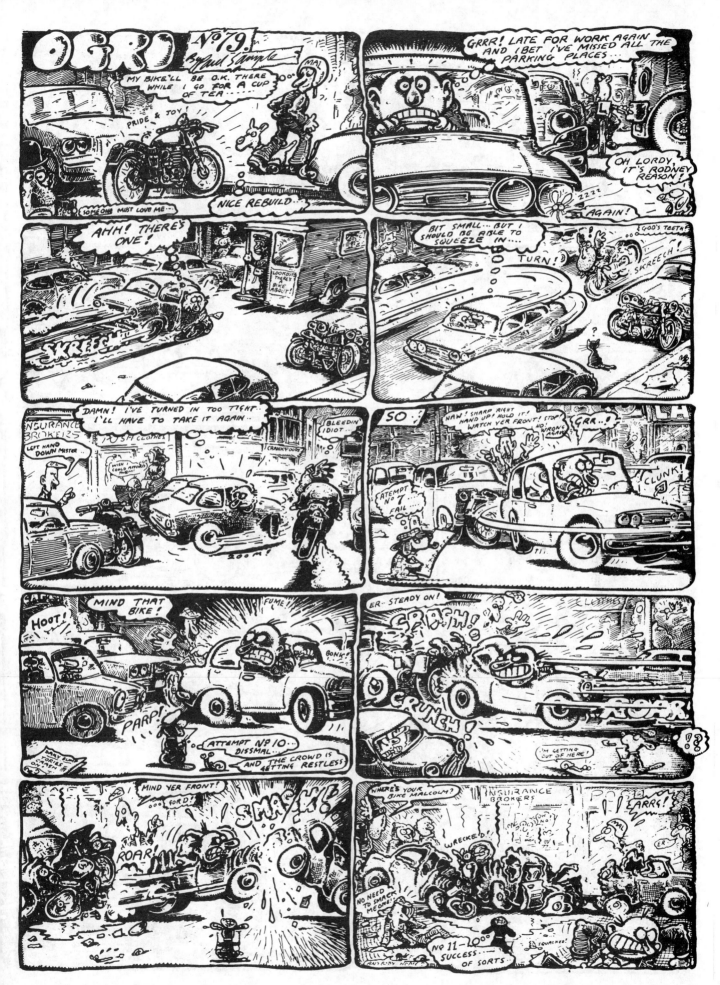

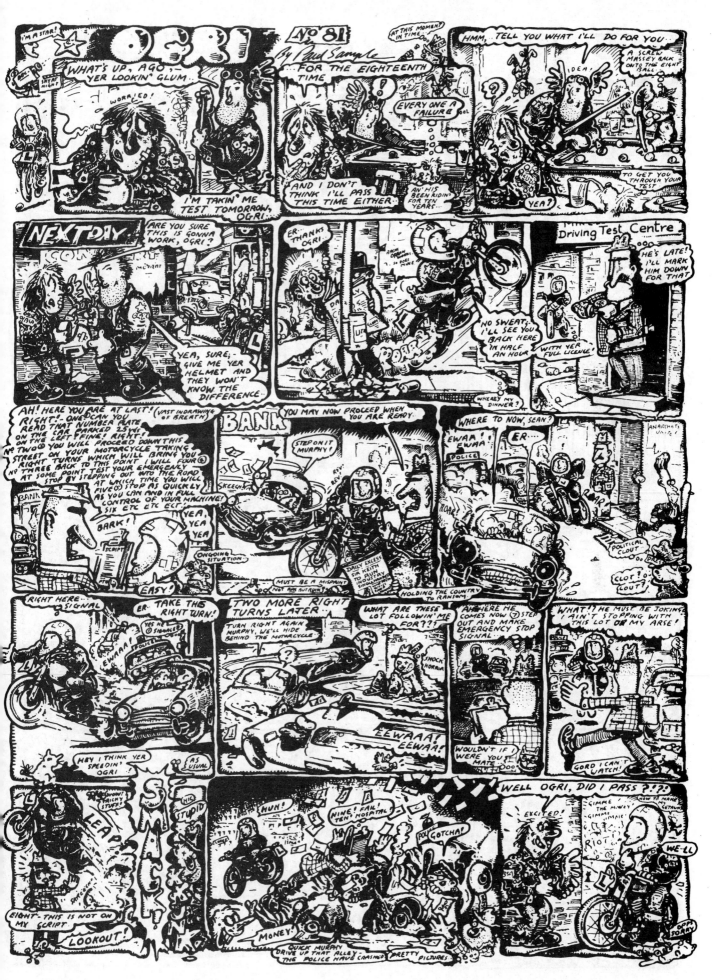

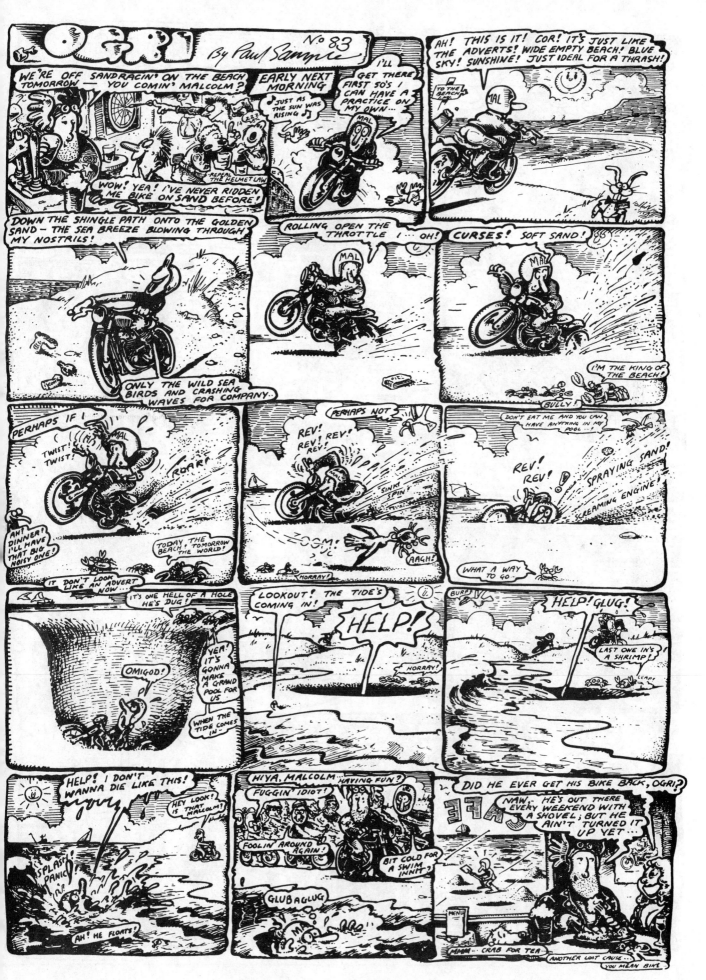

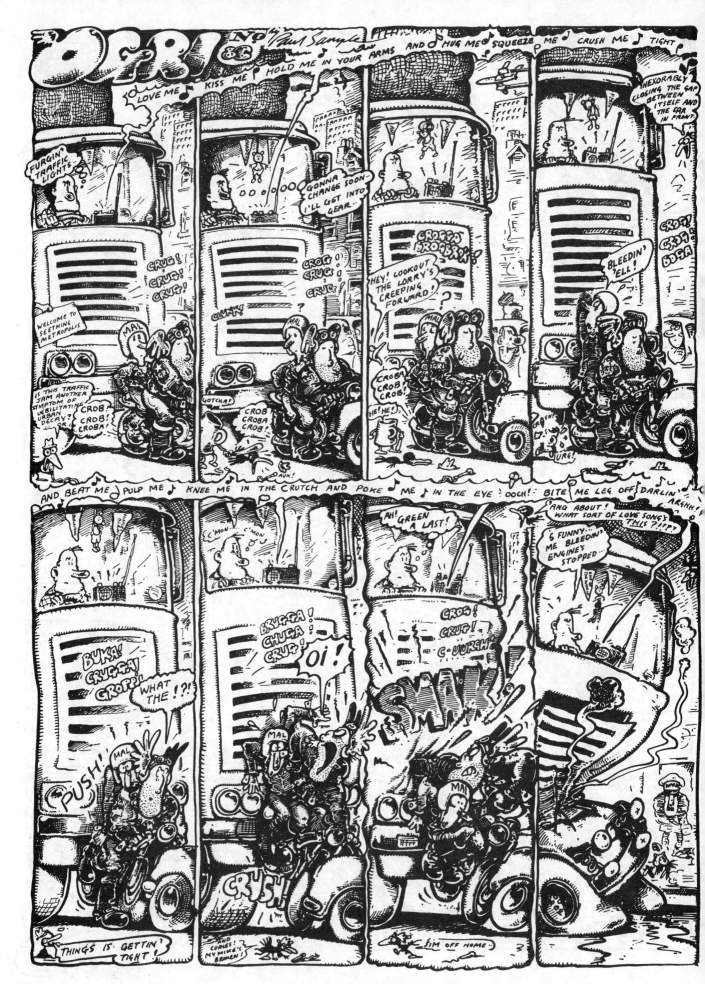

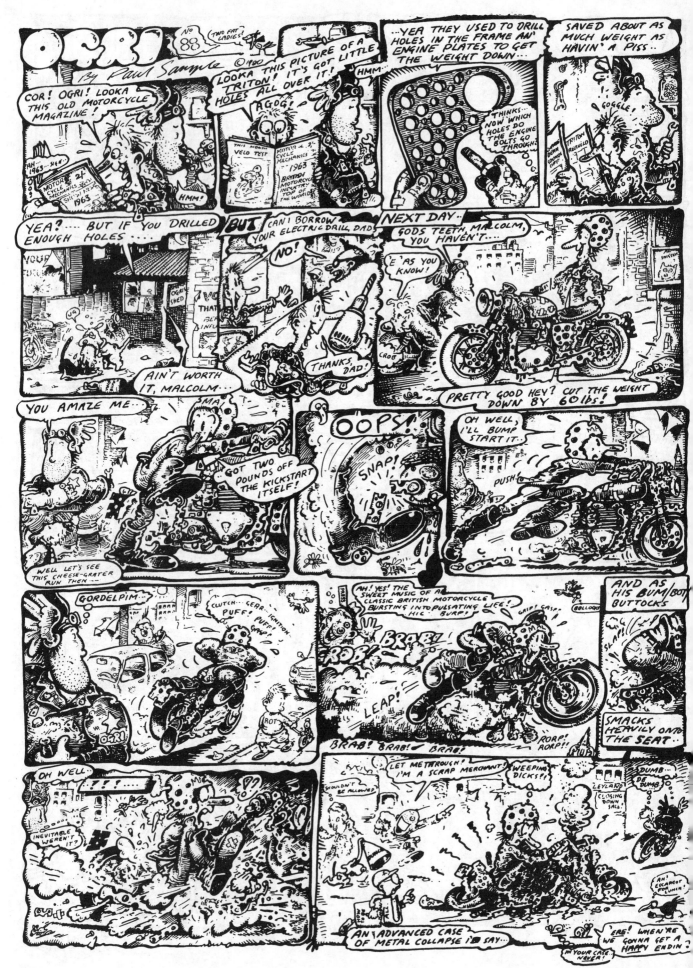

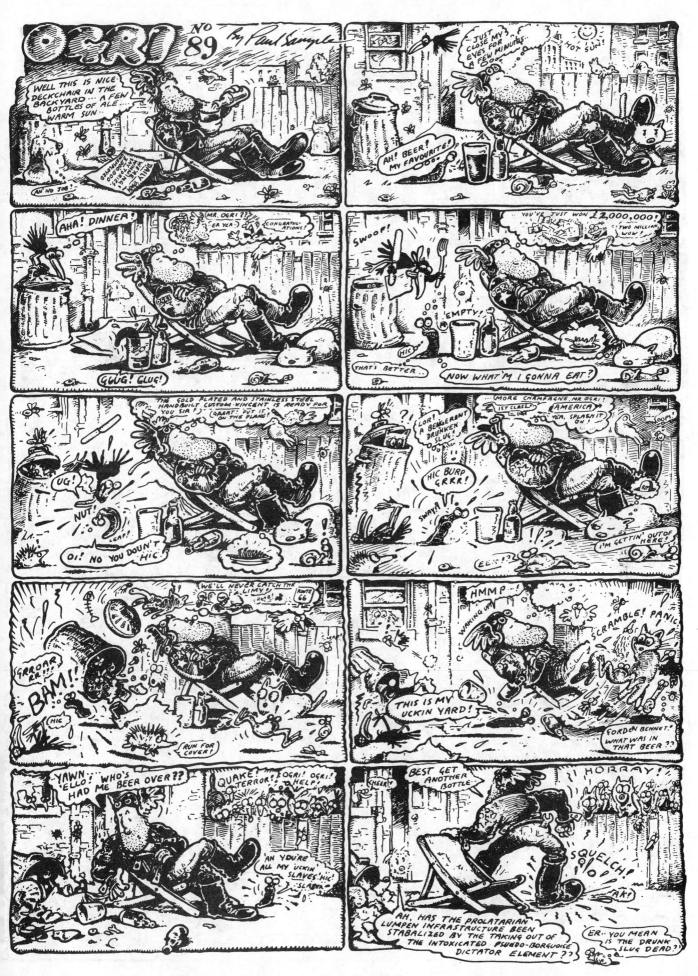

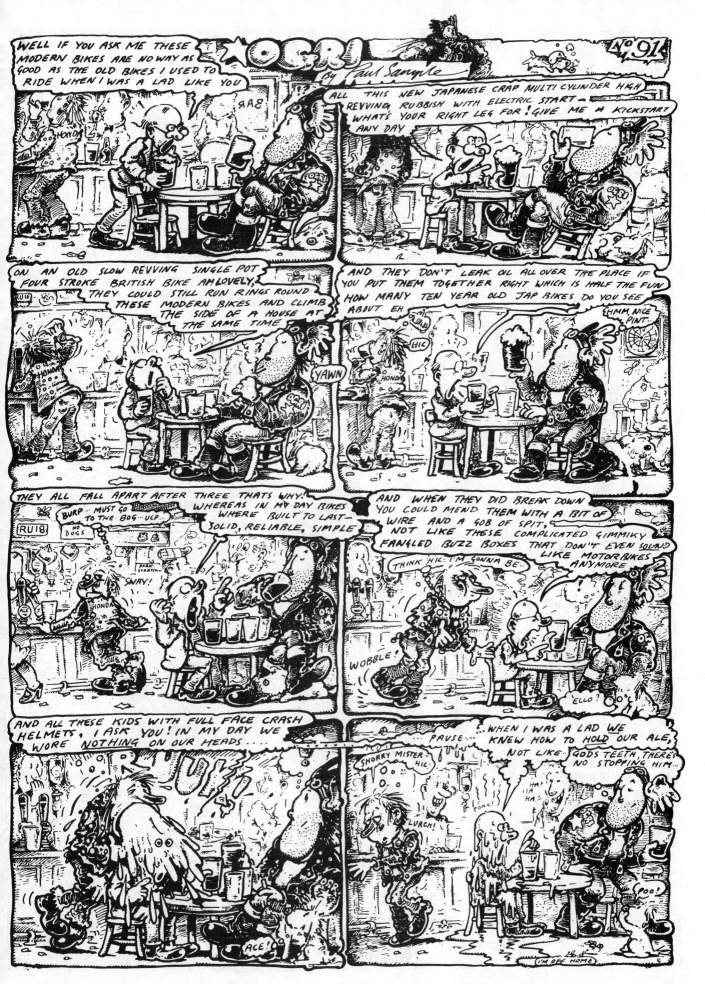

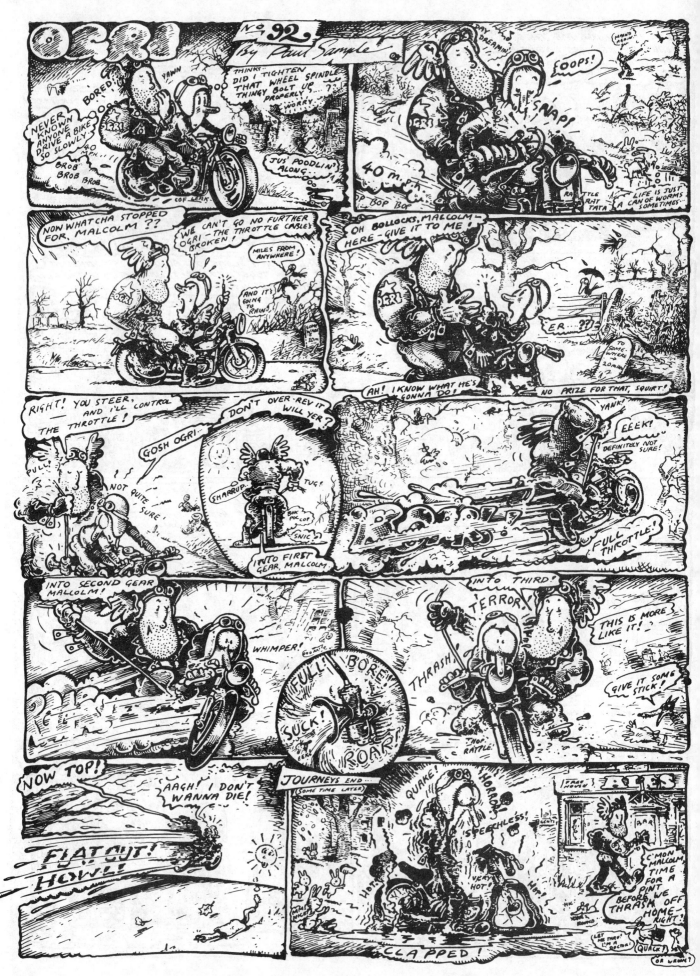

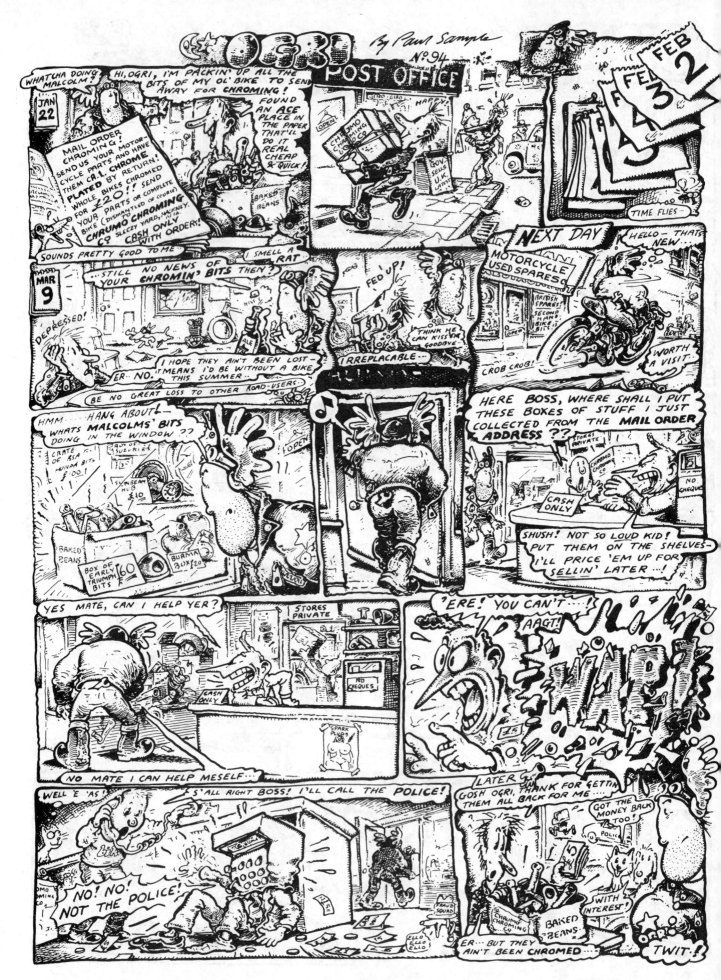

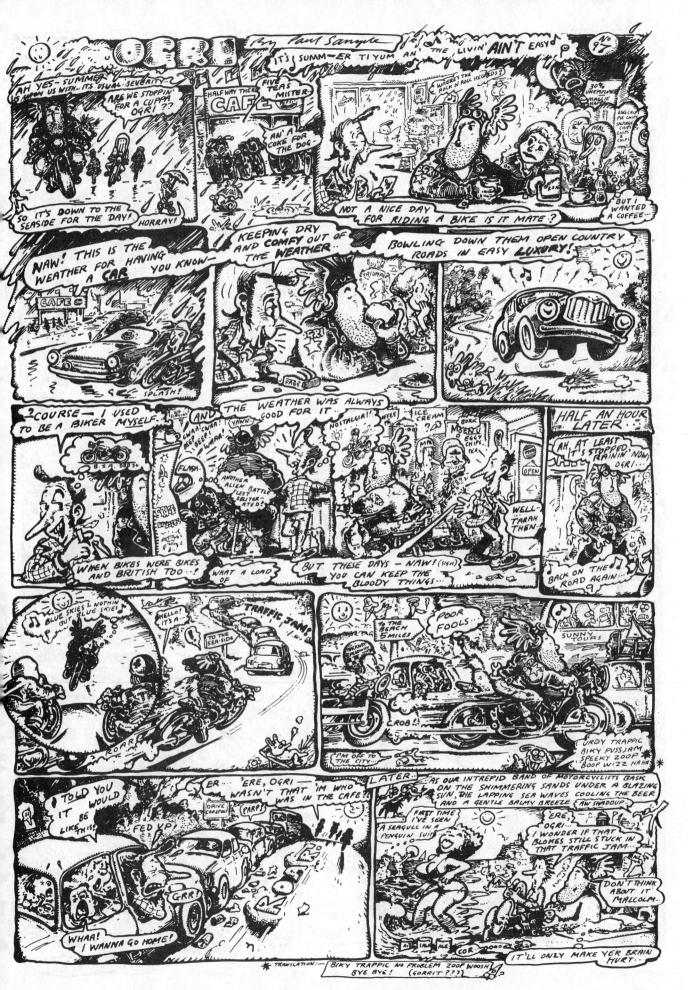

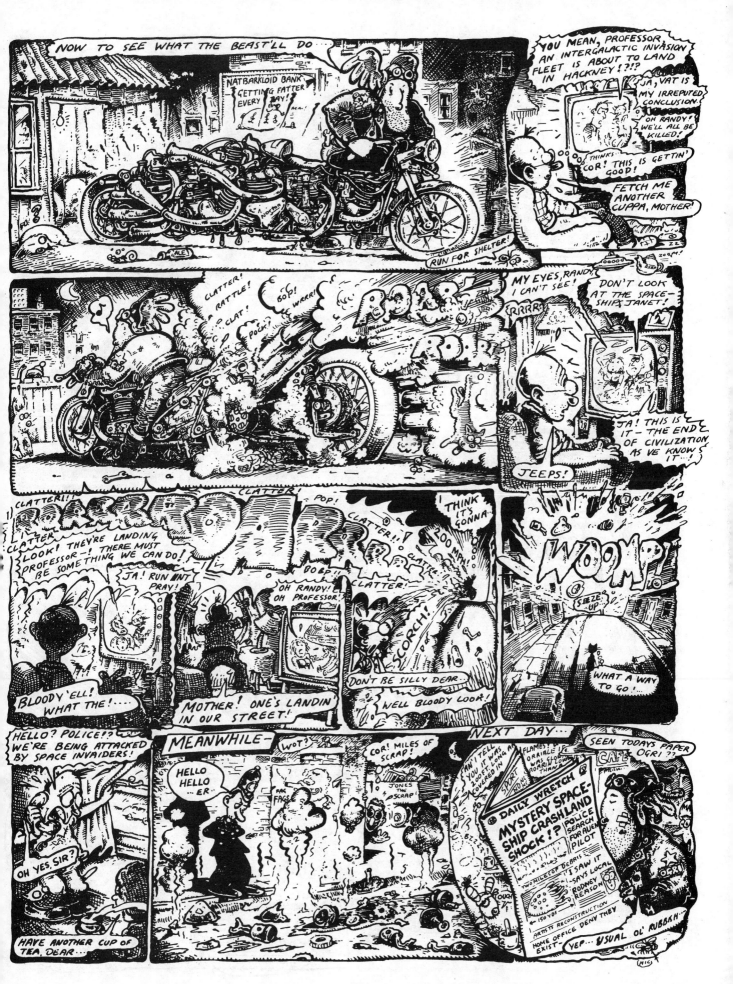

115

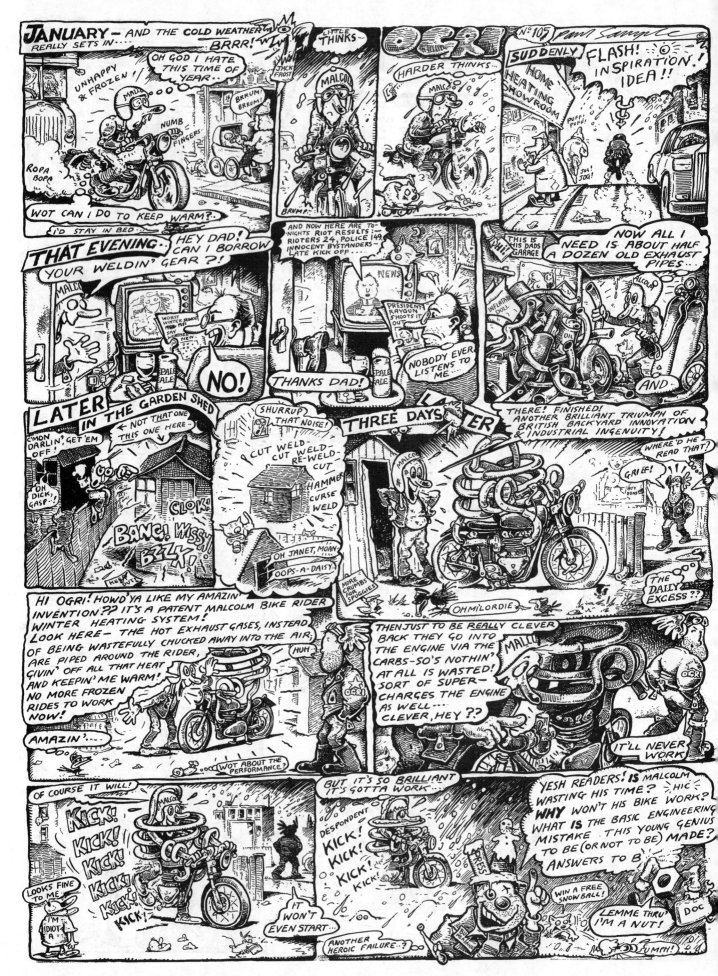

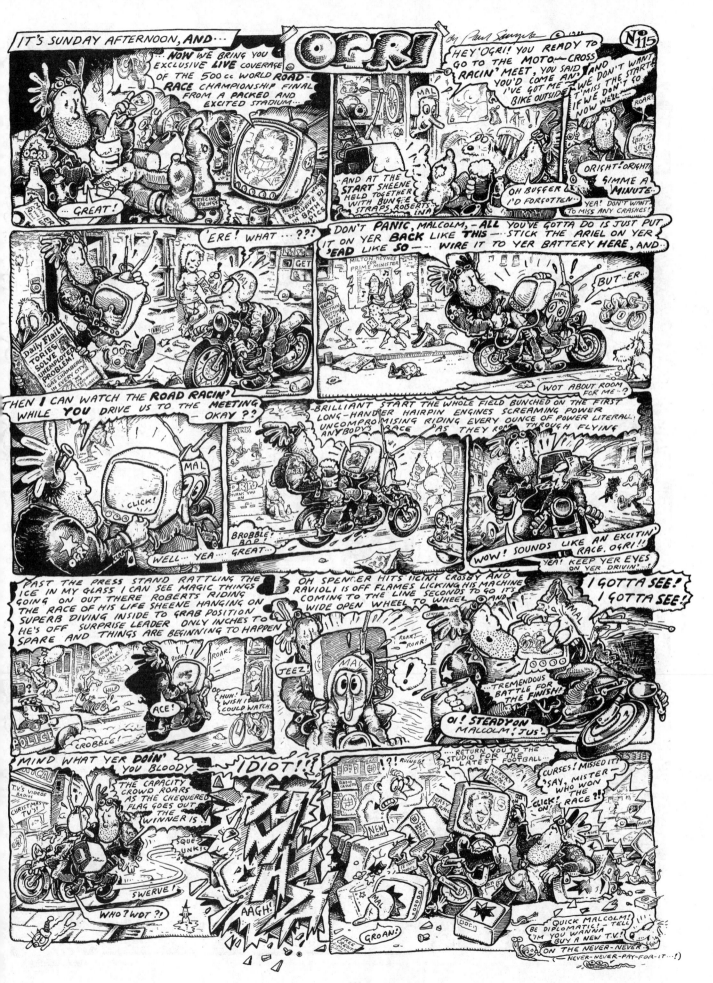

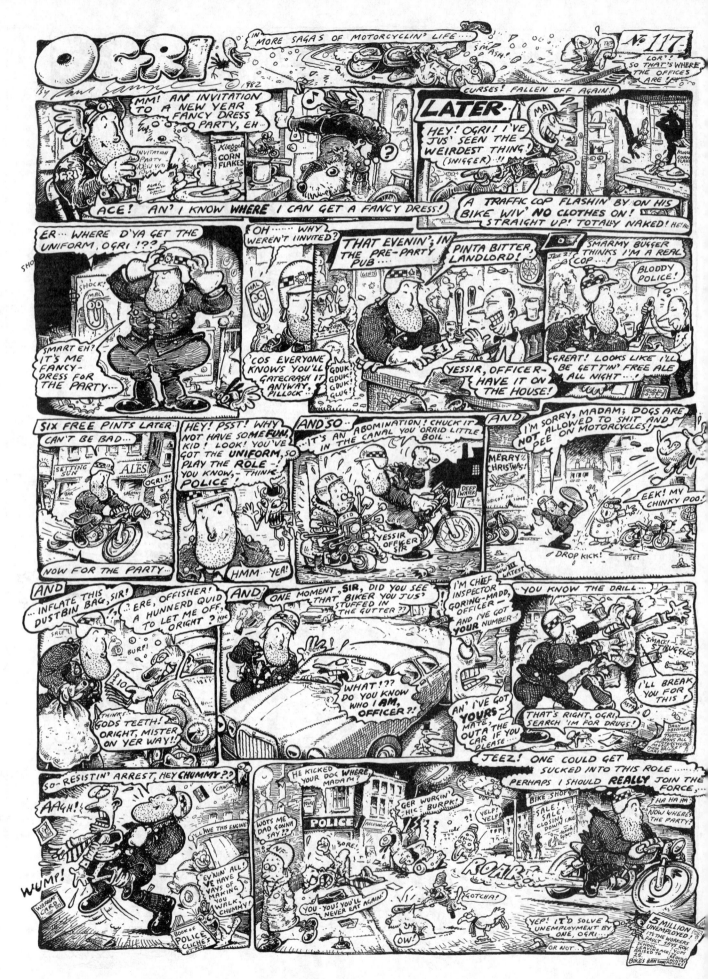

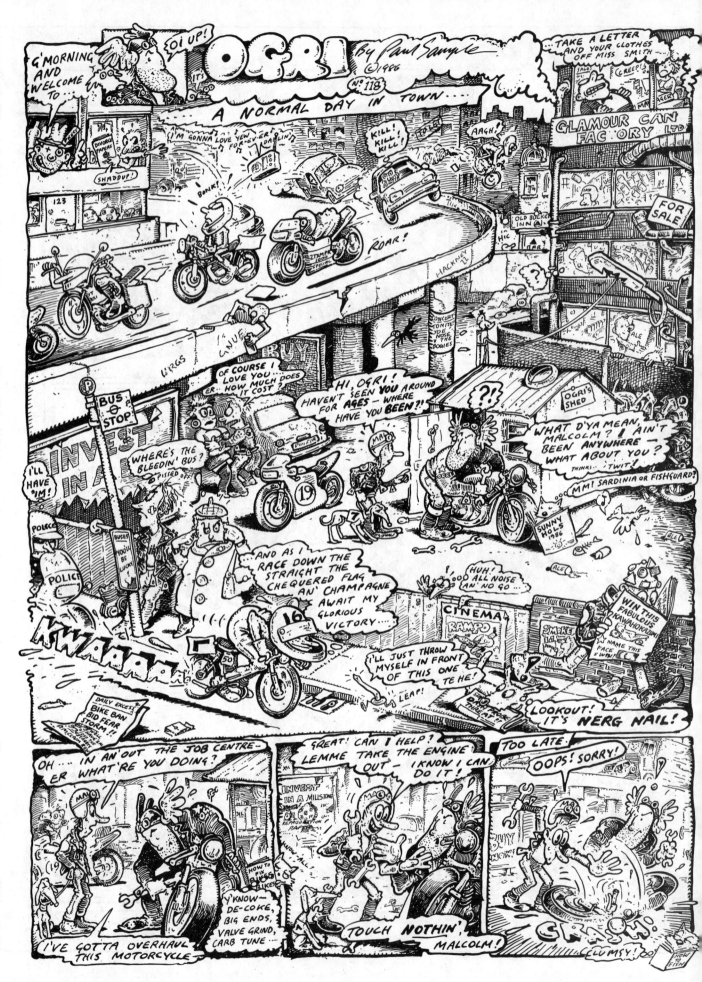

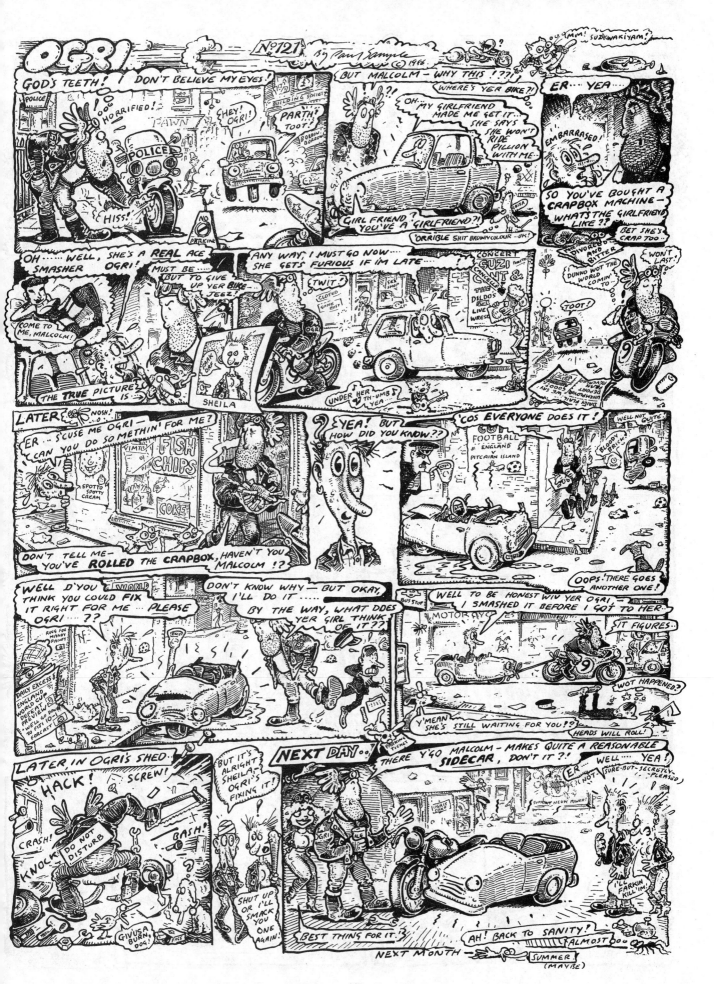

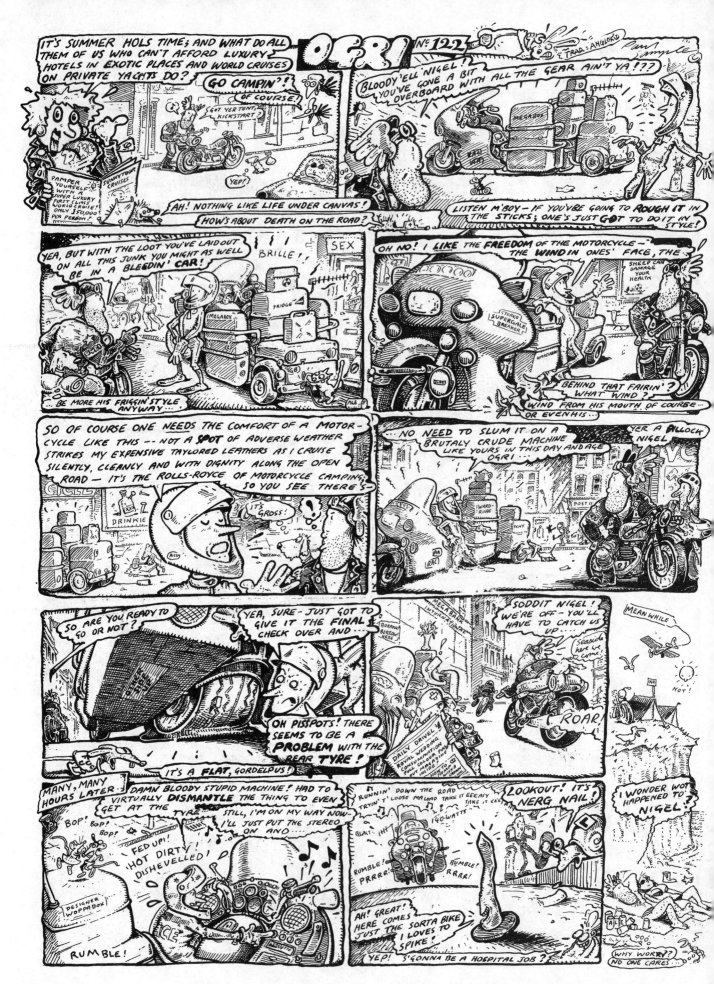

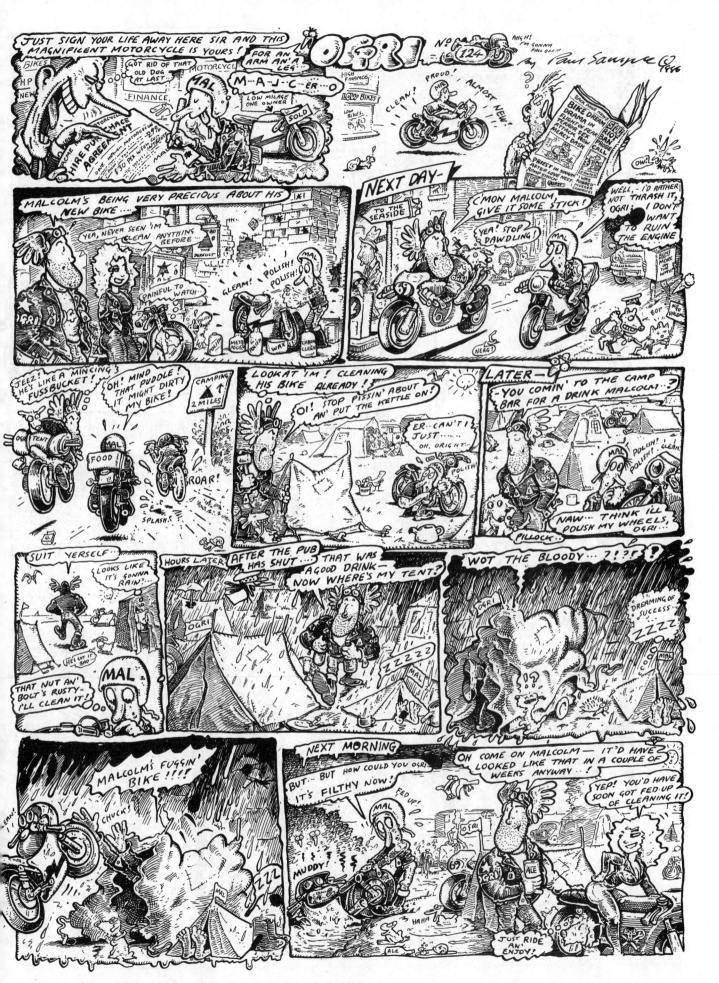

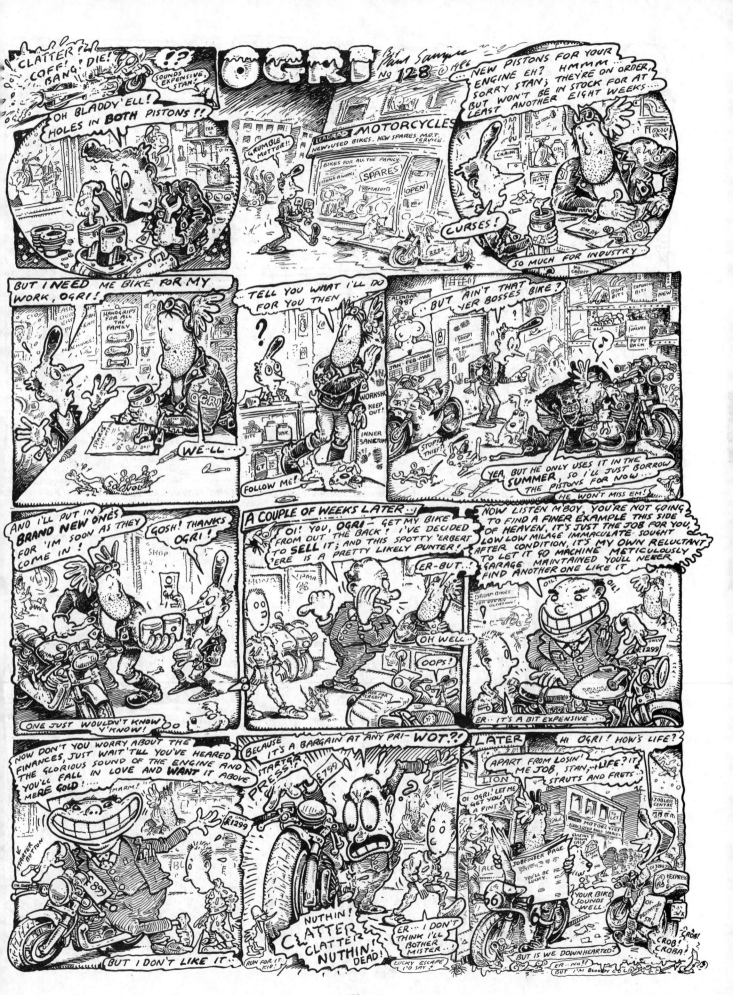

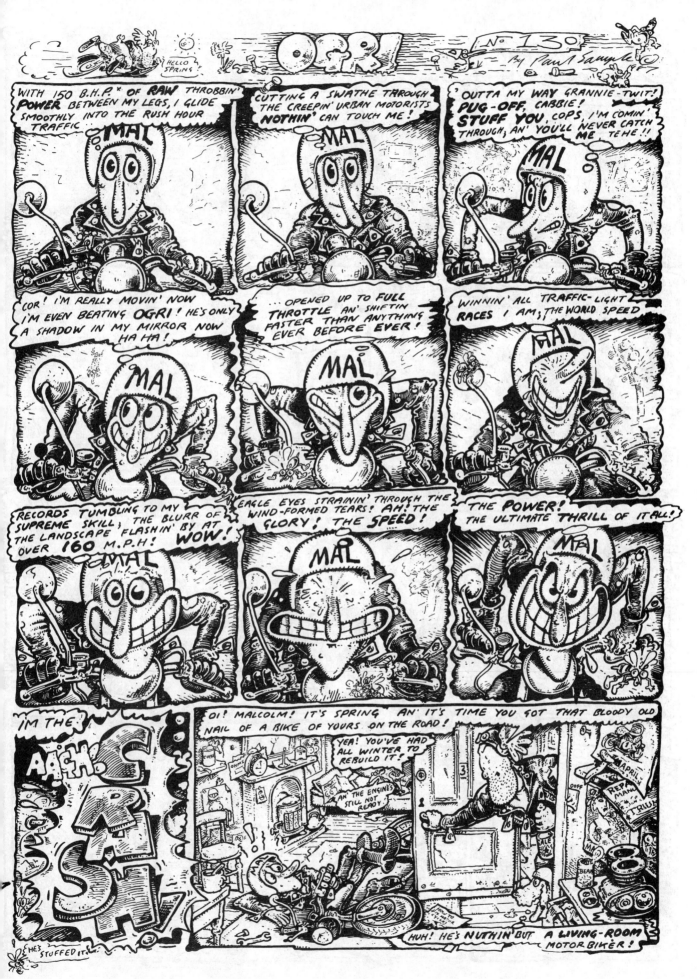

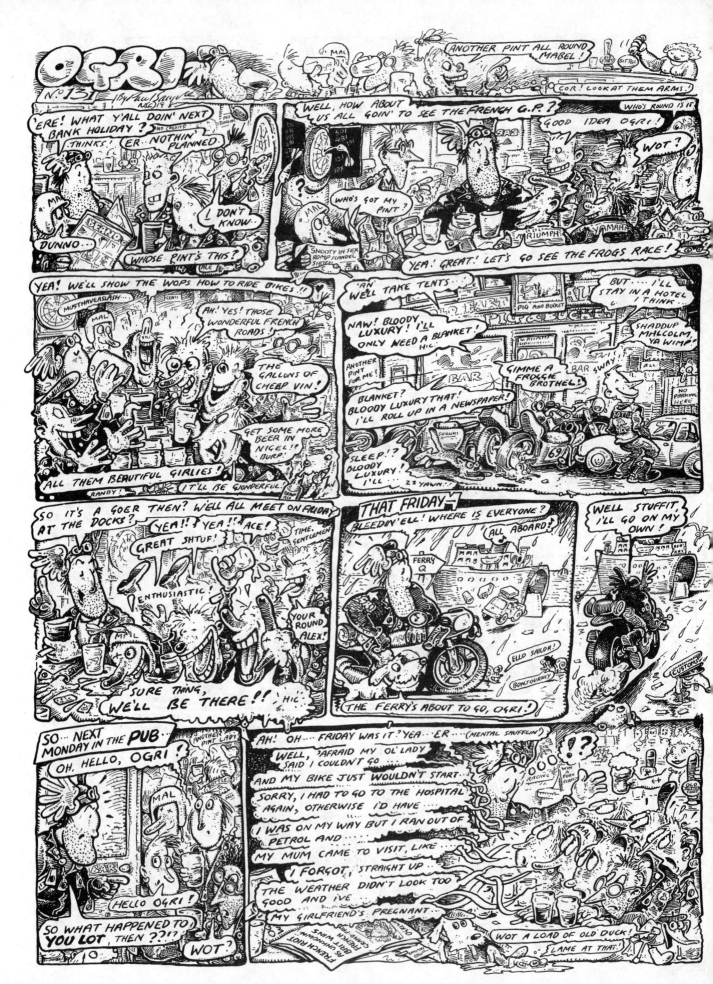

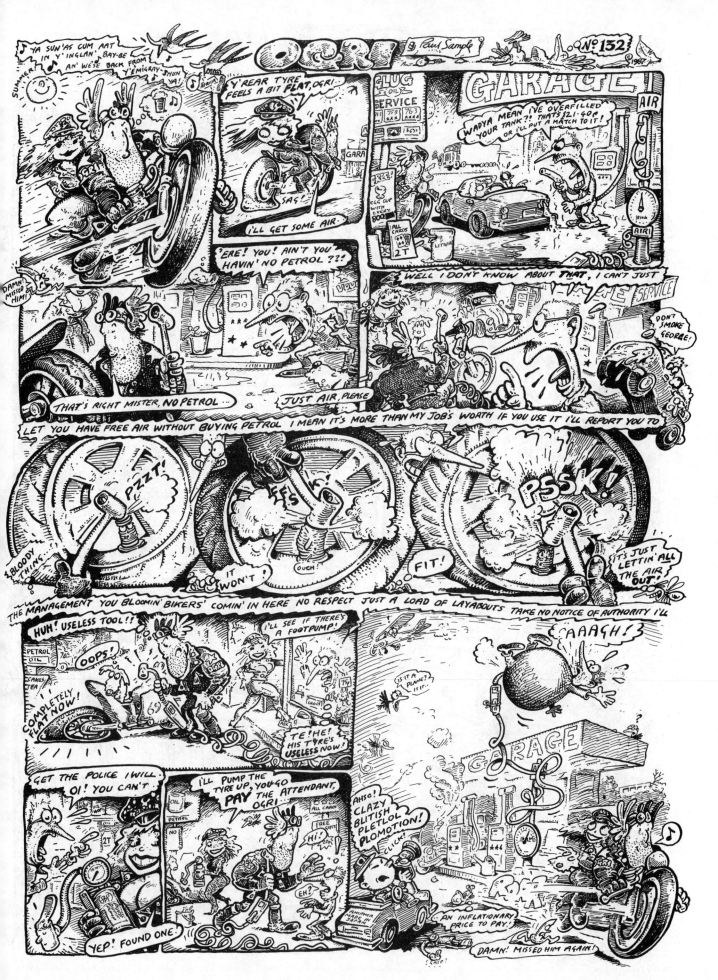

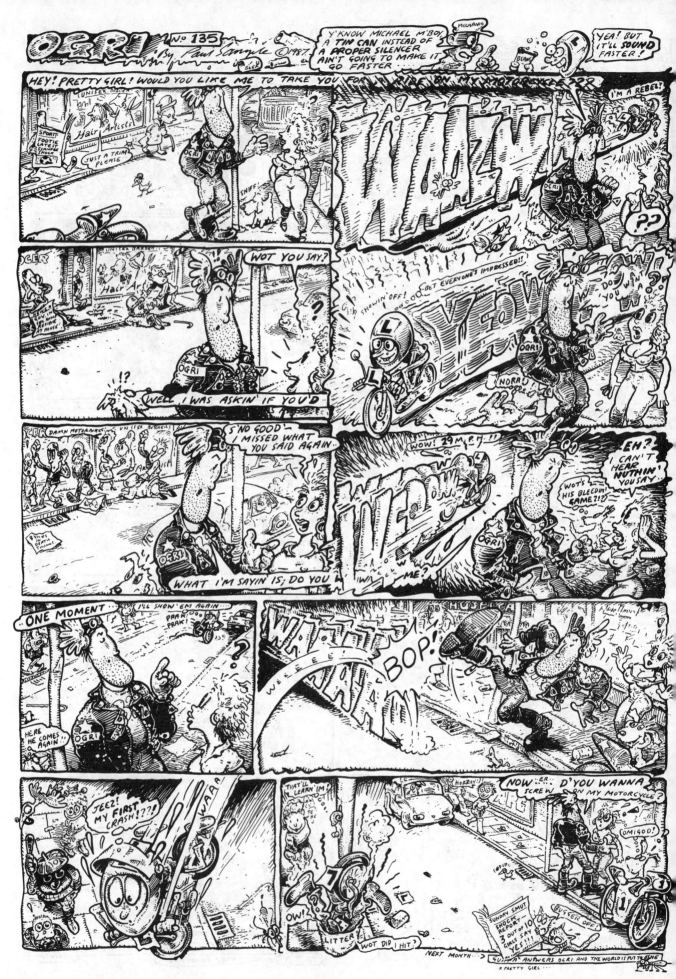

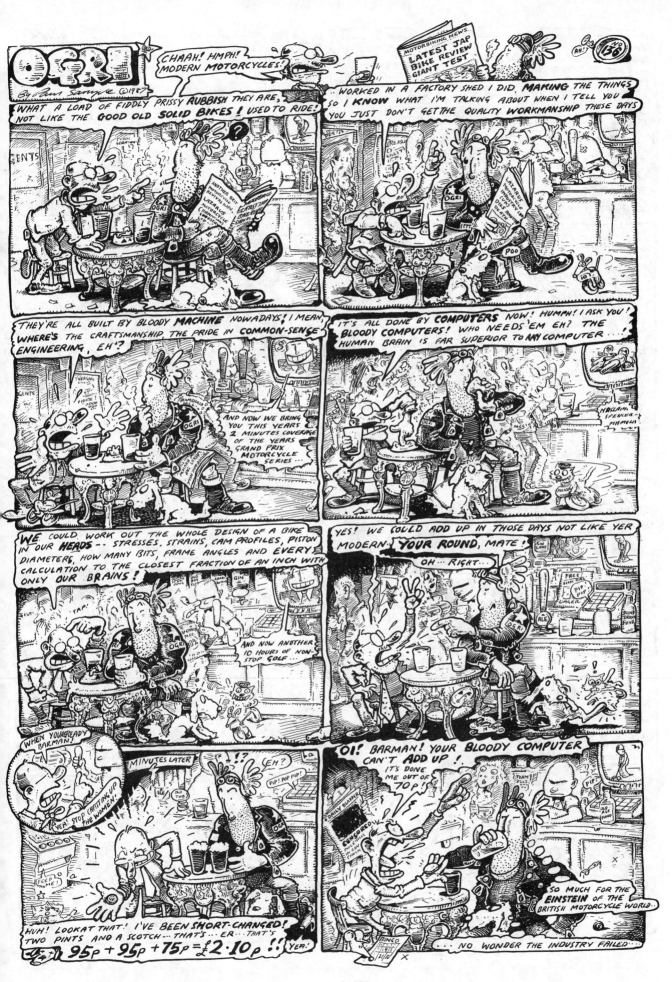

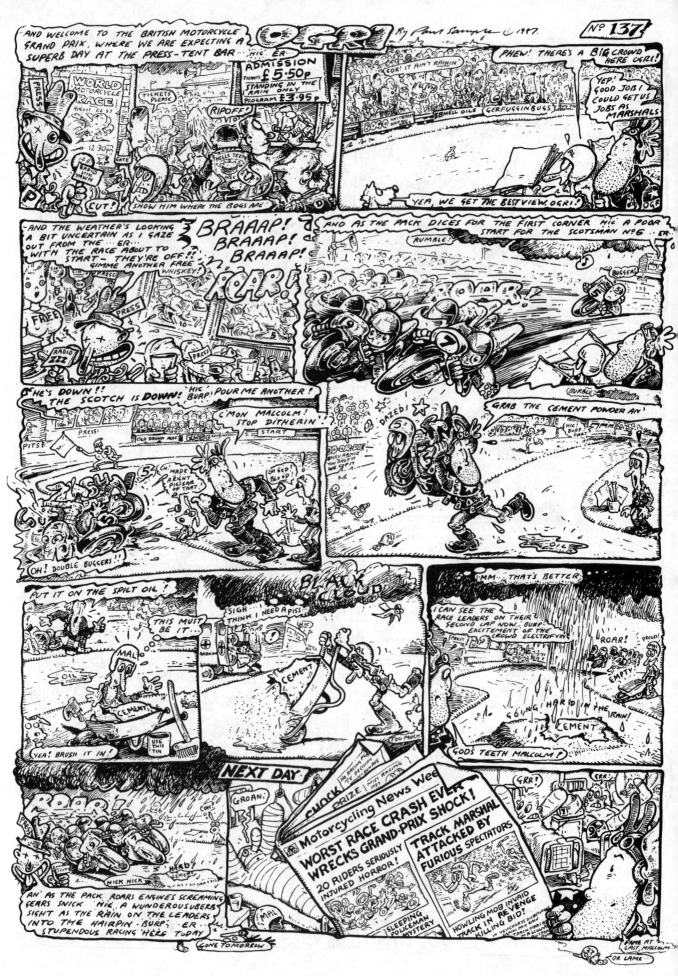

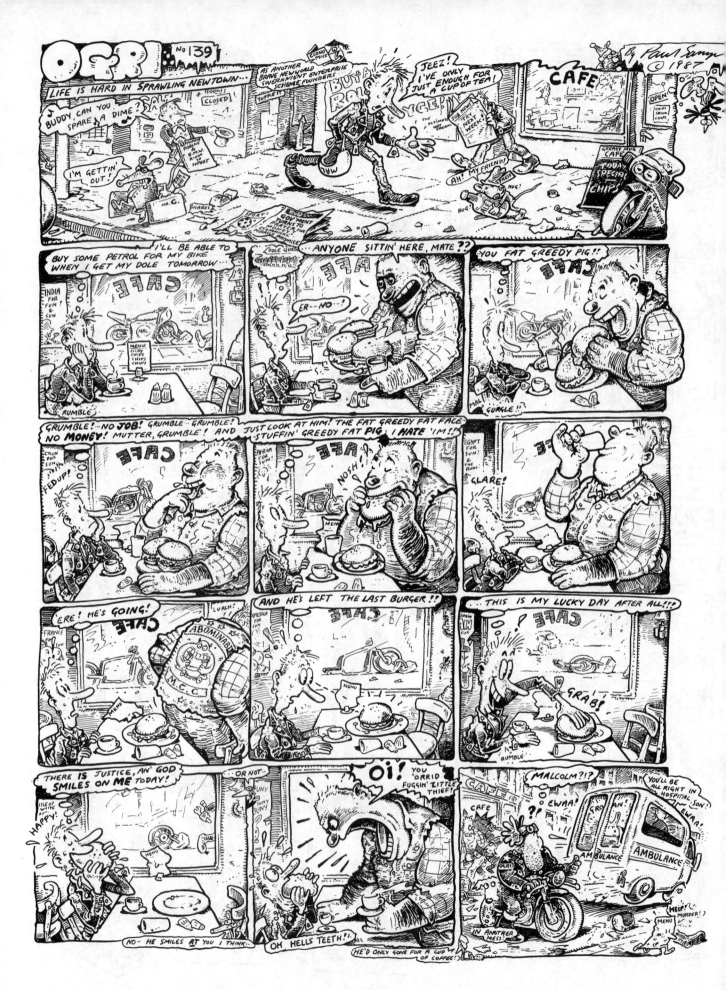

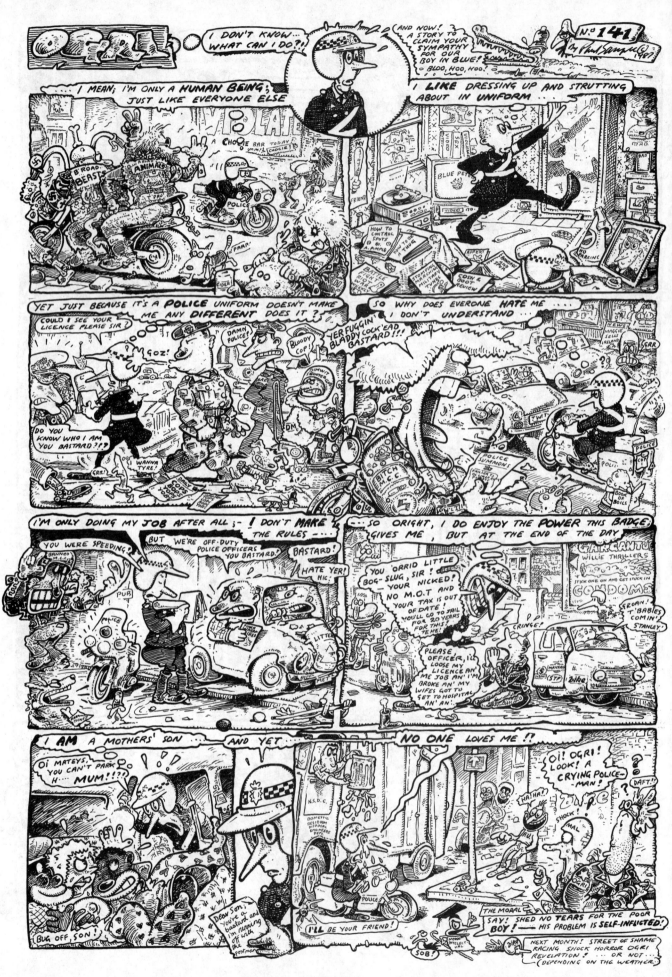

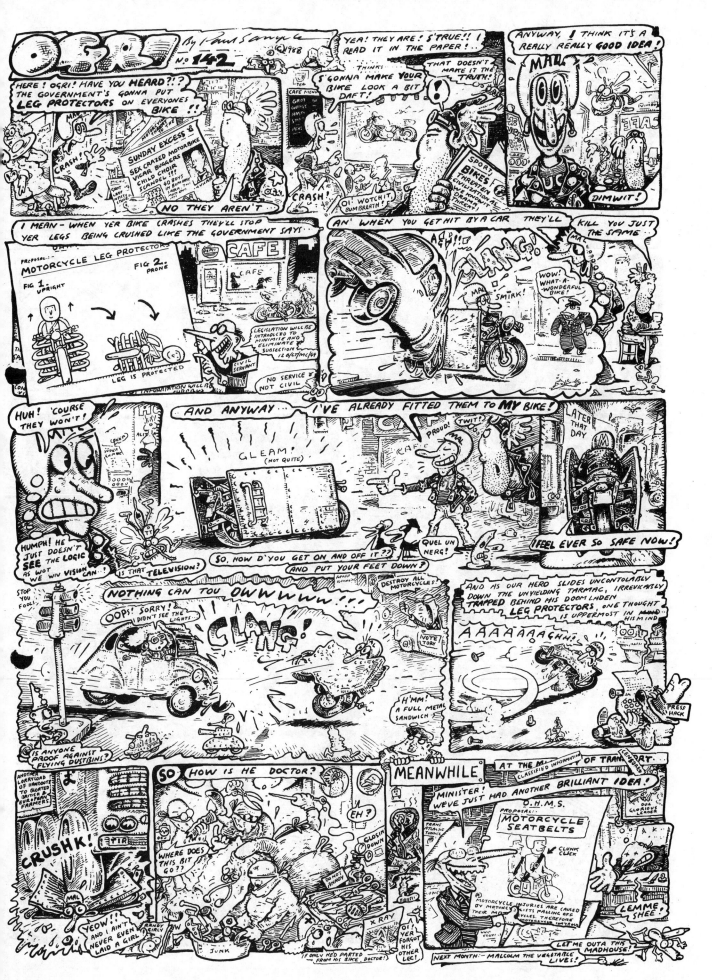

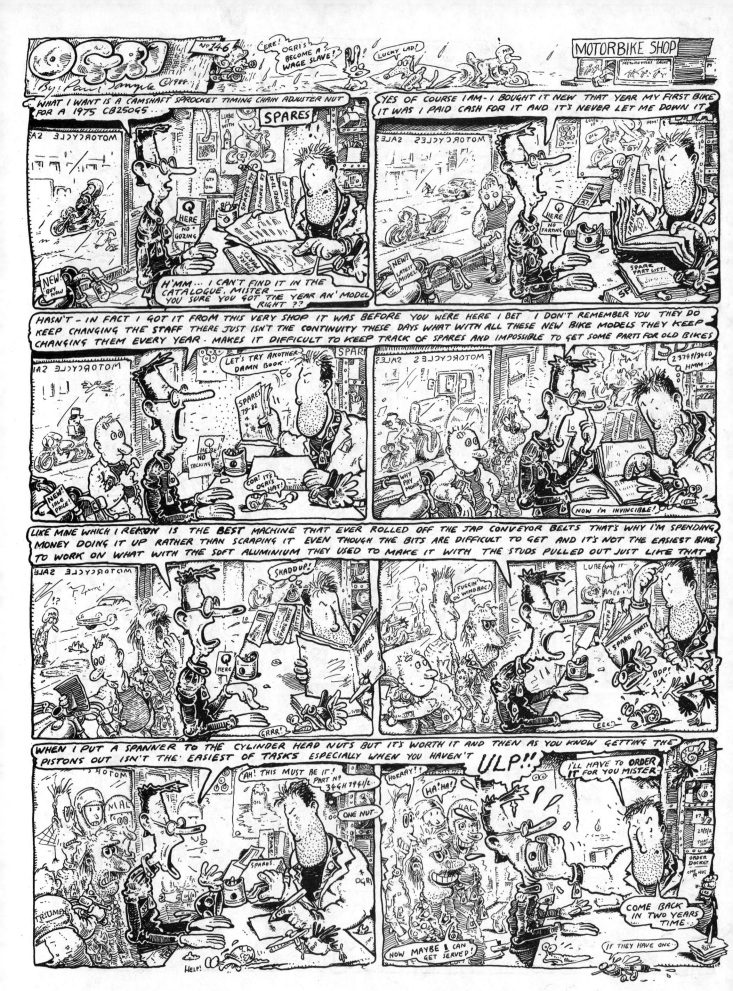

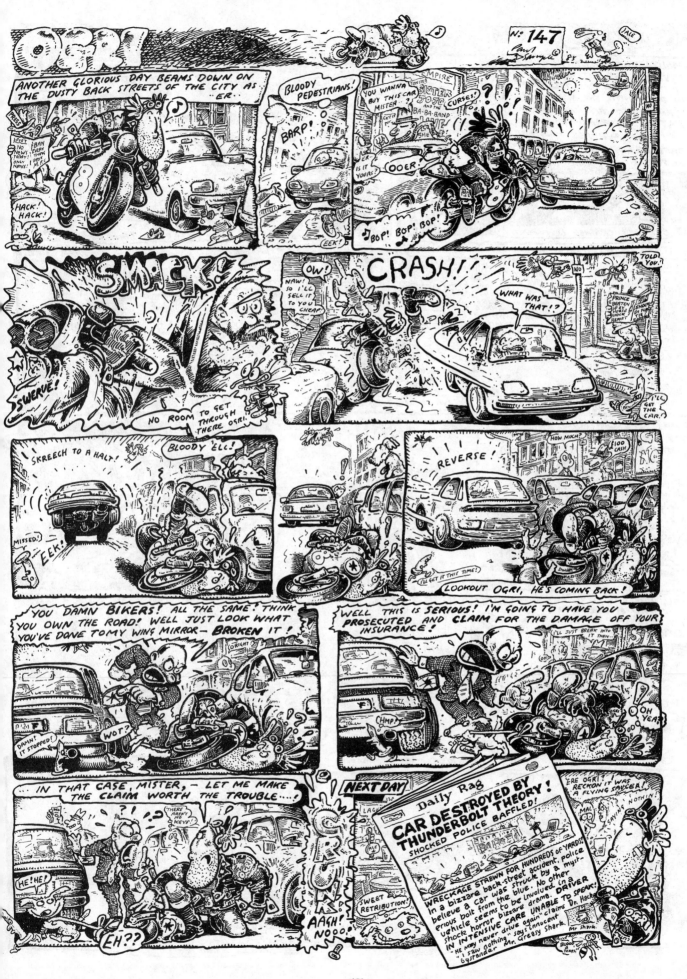

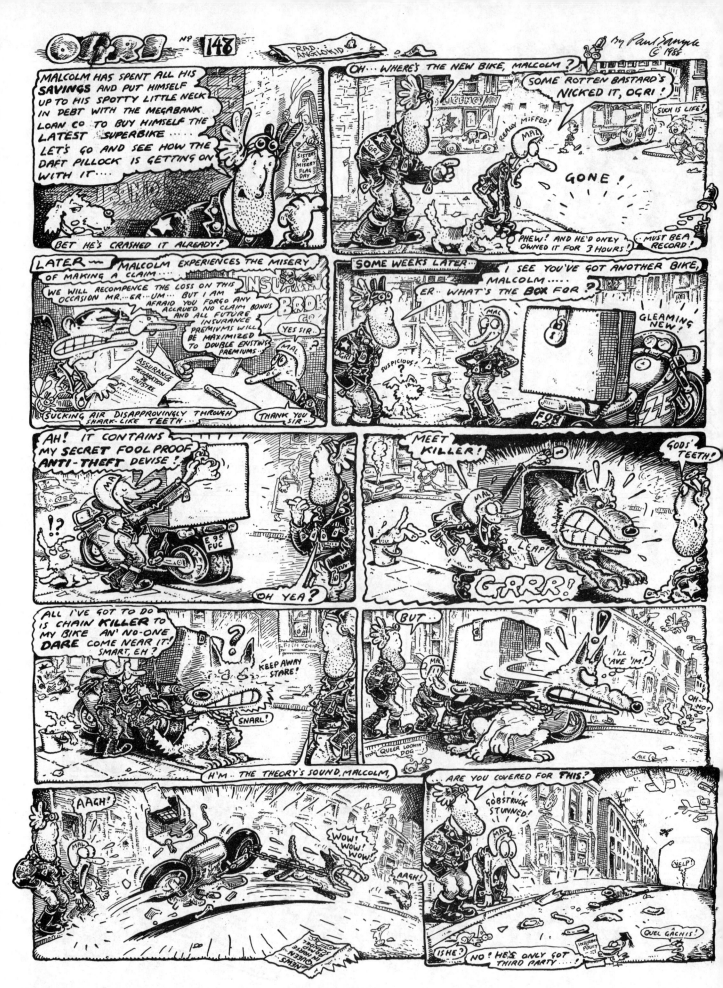

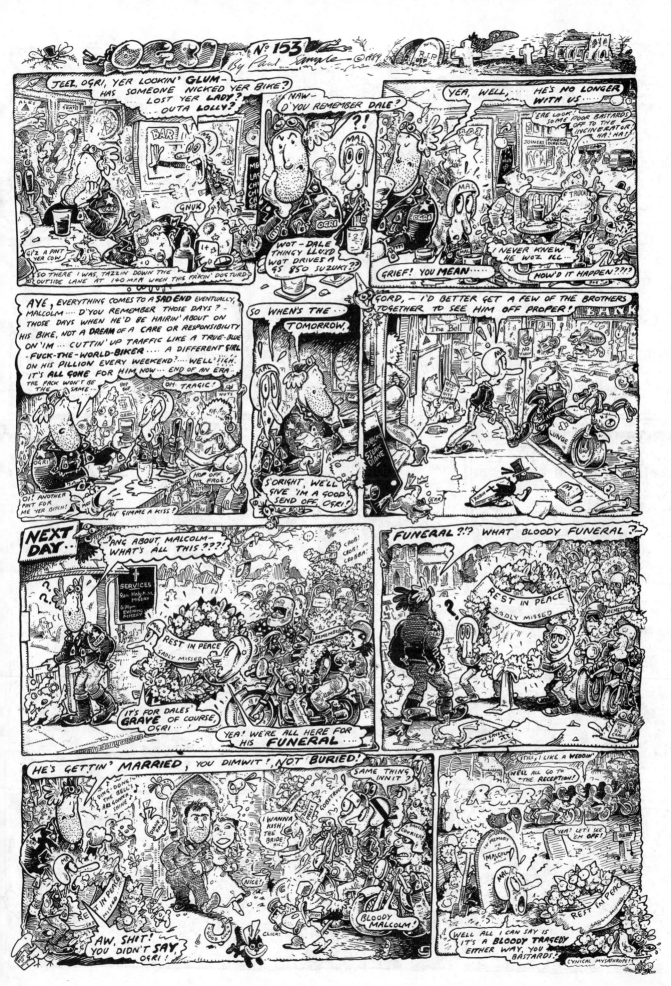

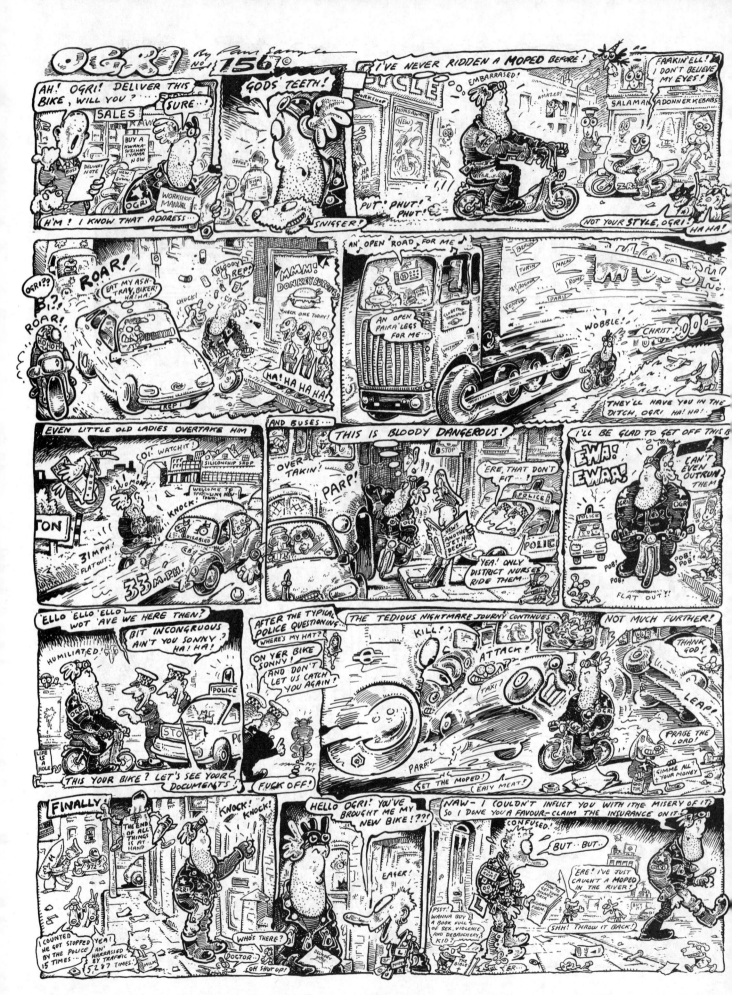

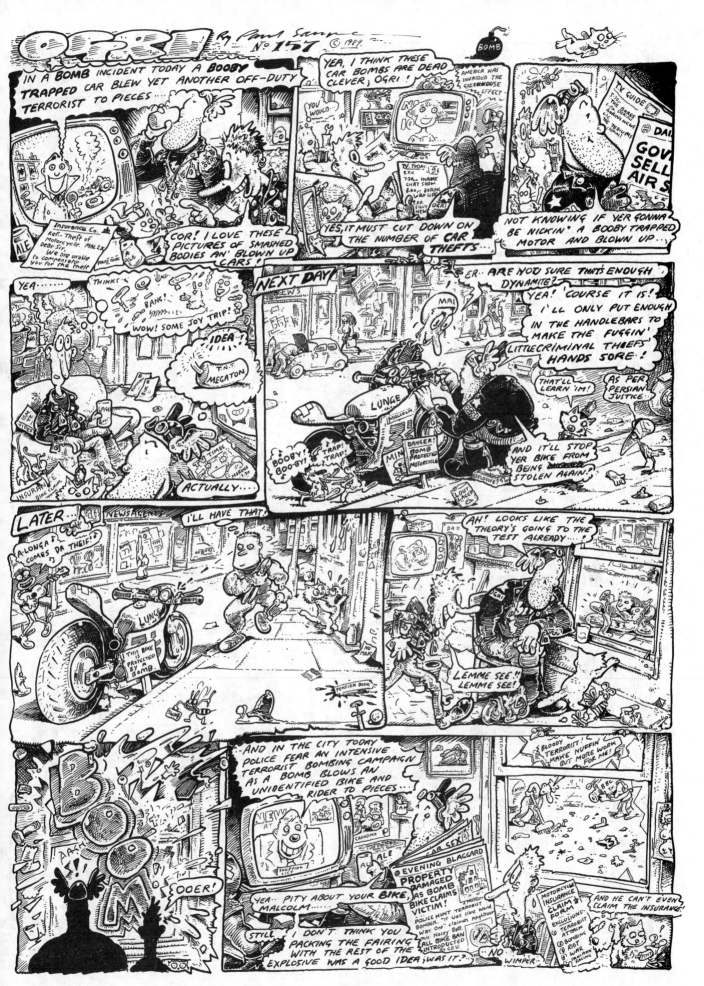

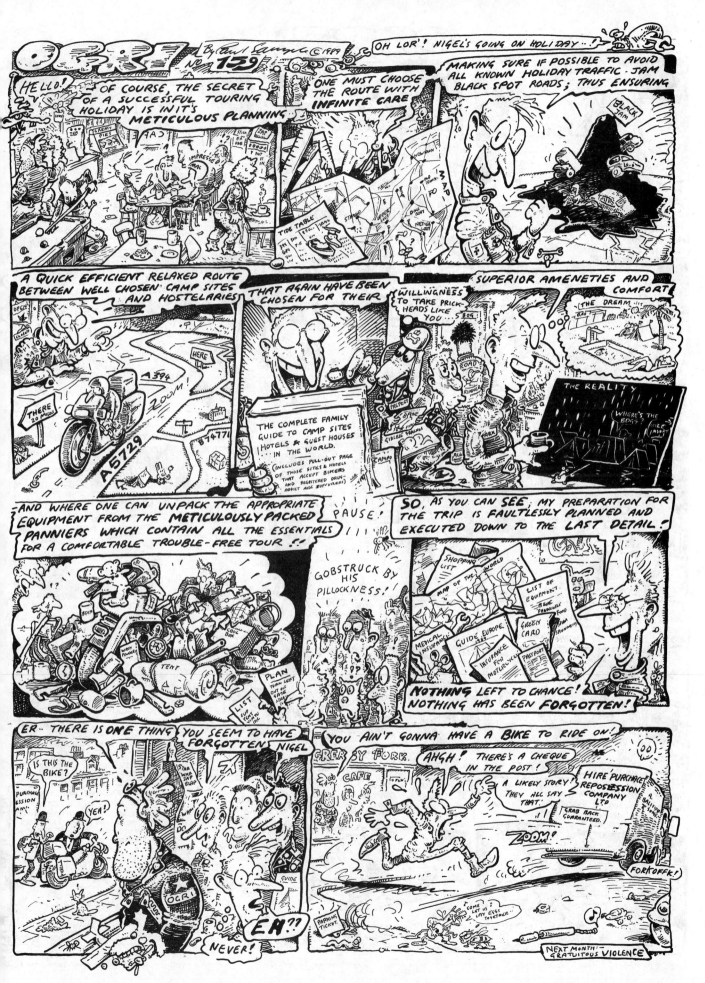

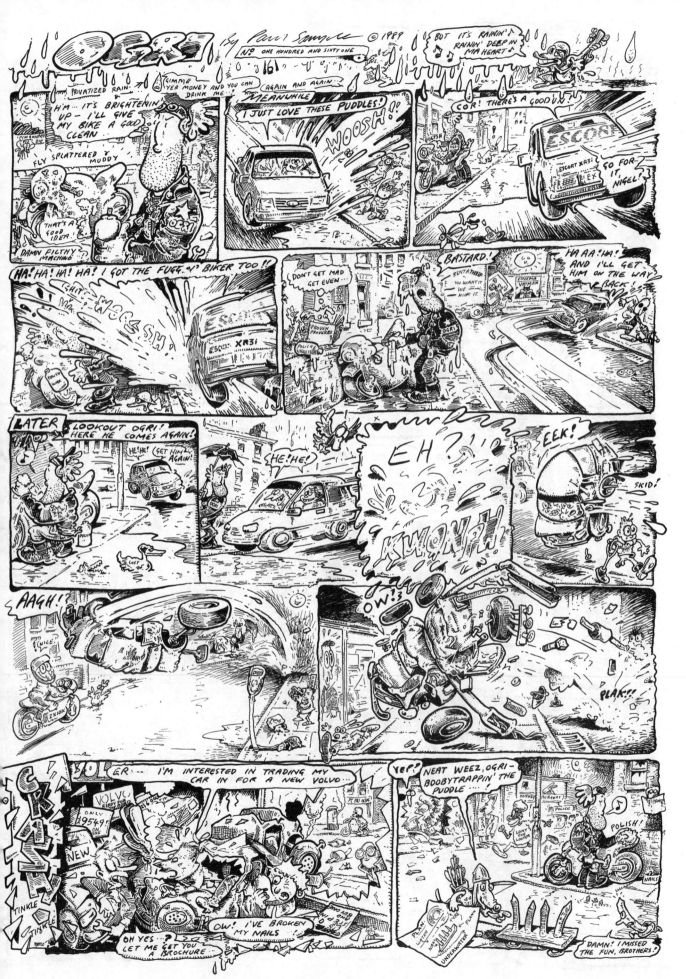

163

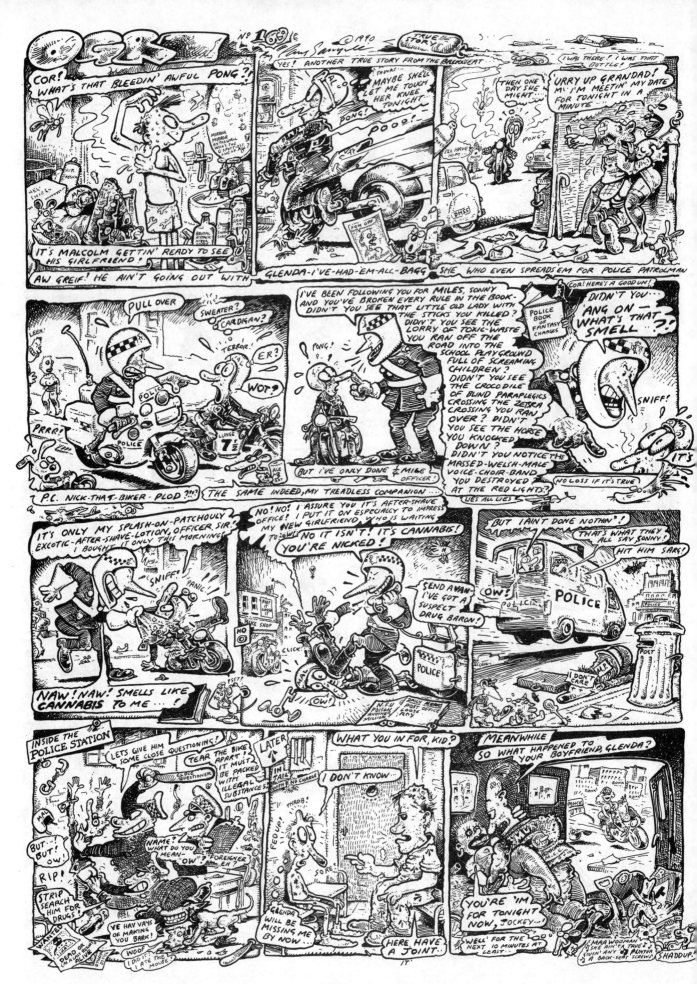

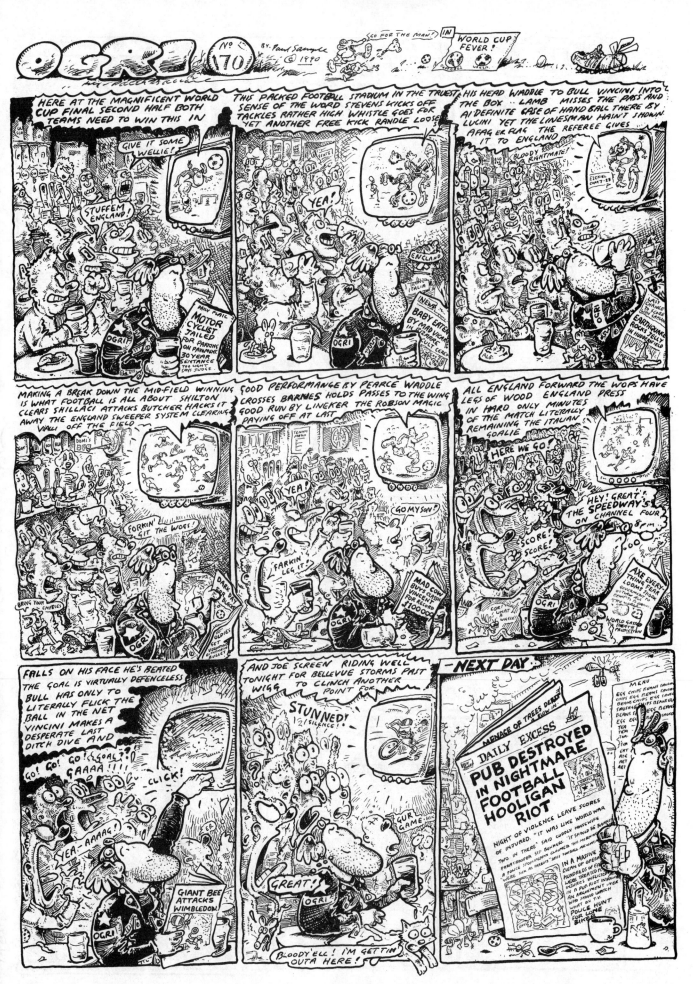

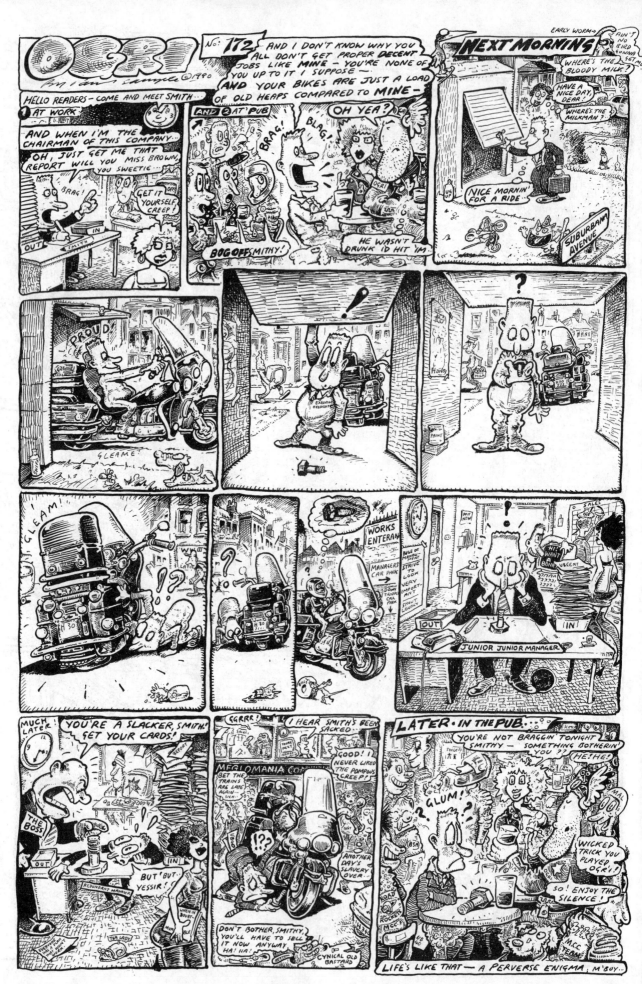

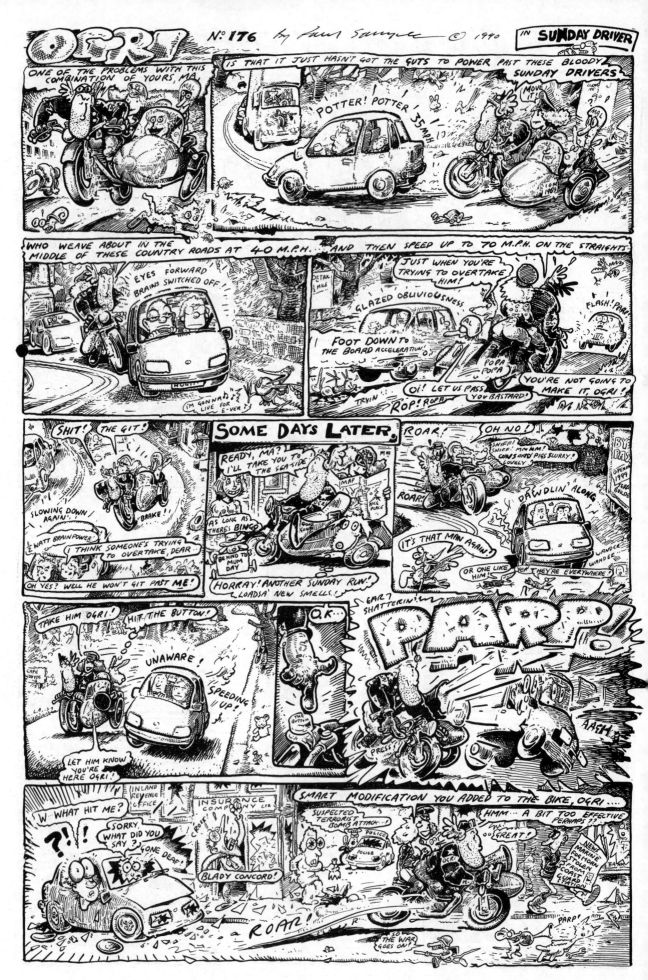

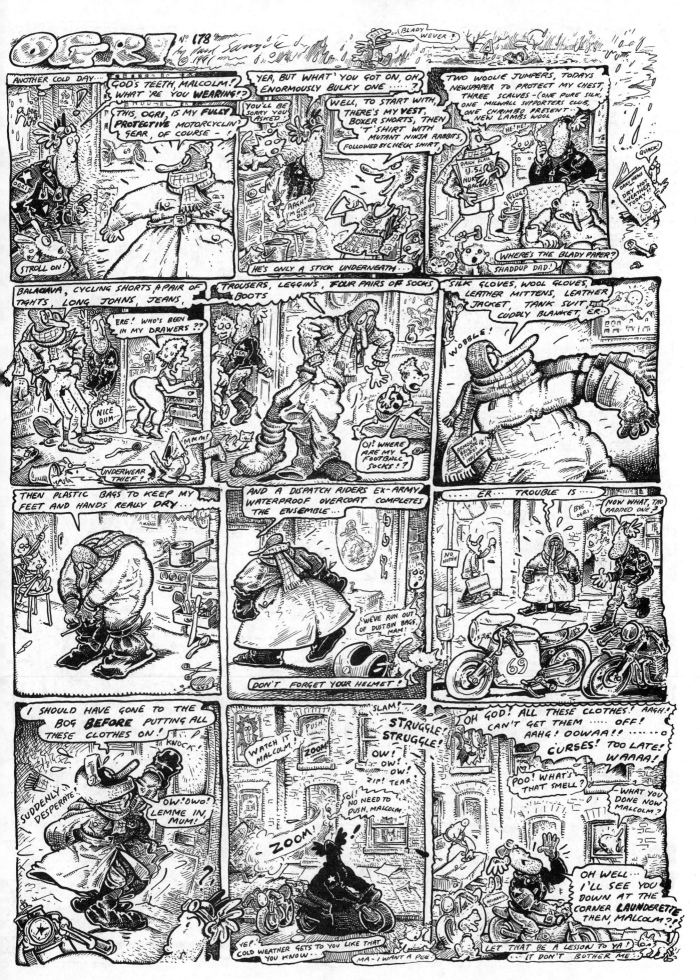

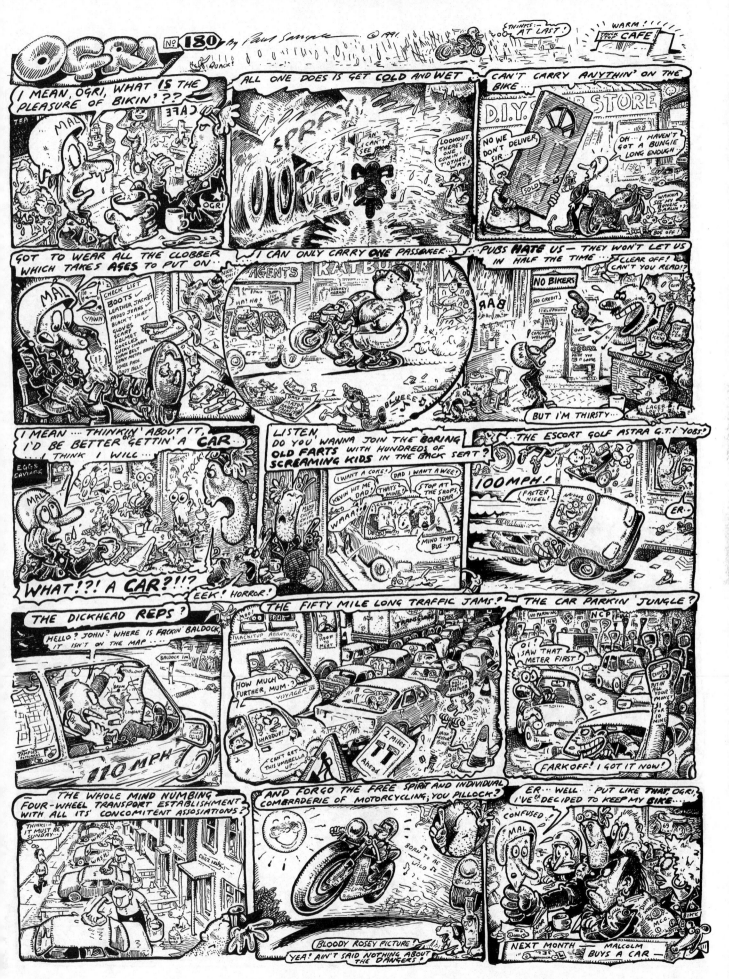

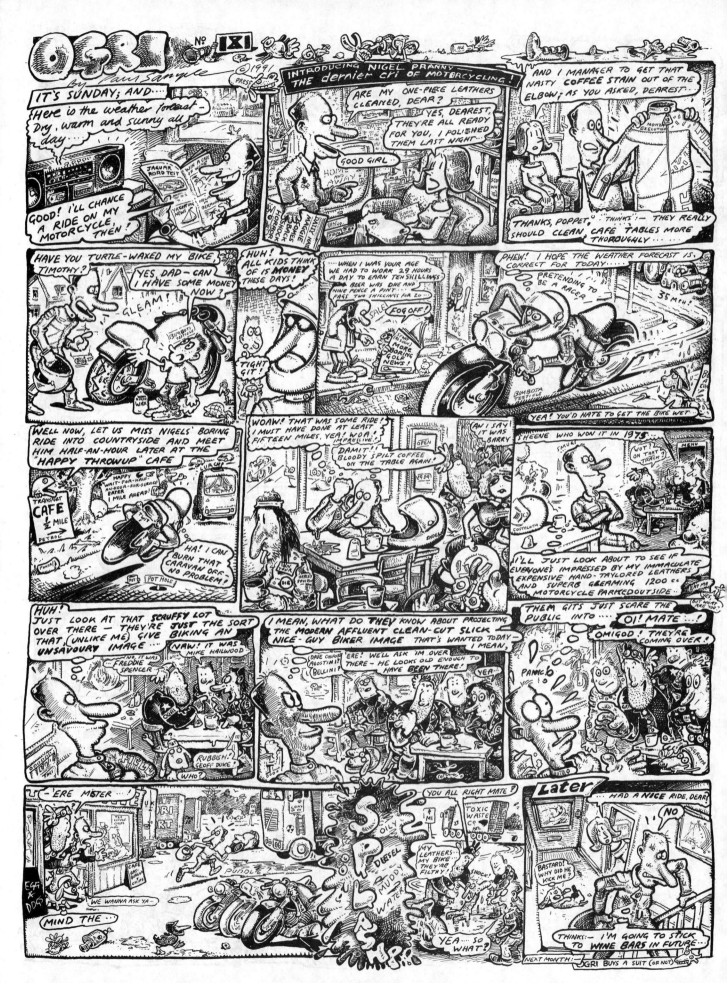

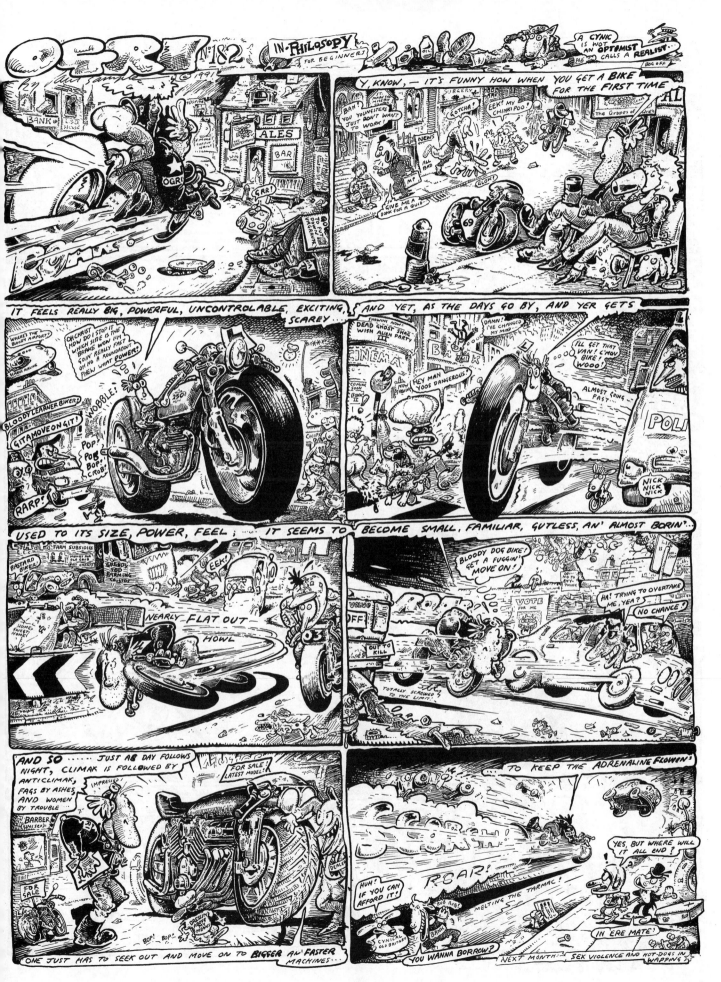

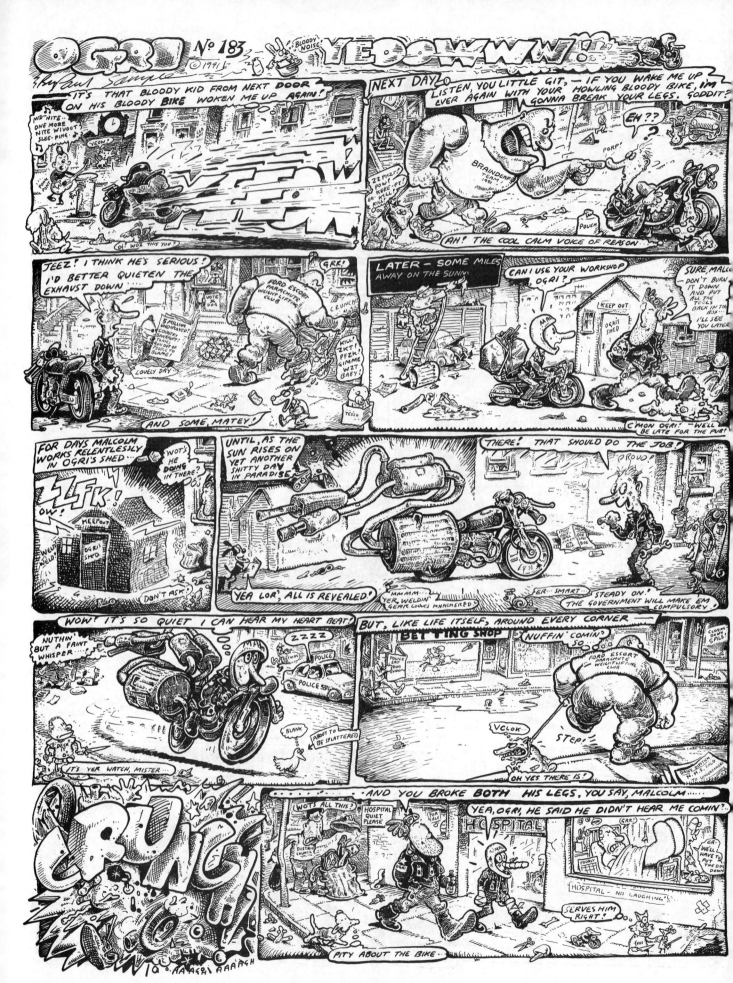

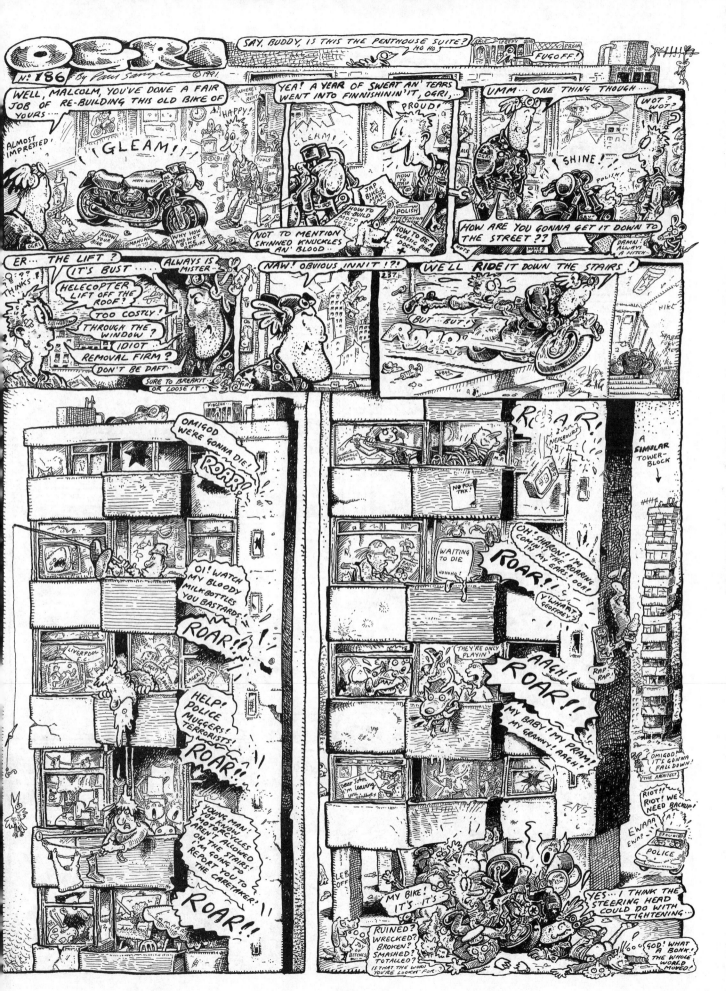

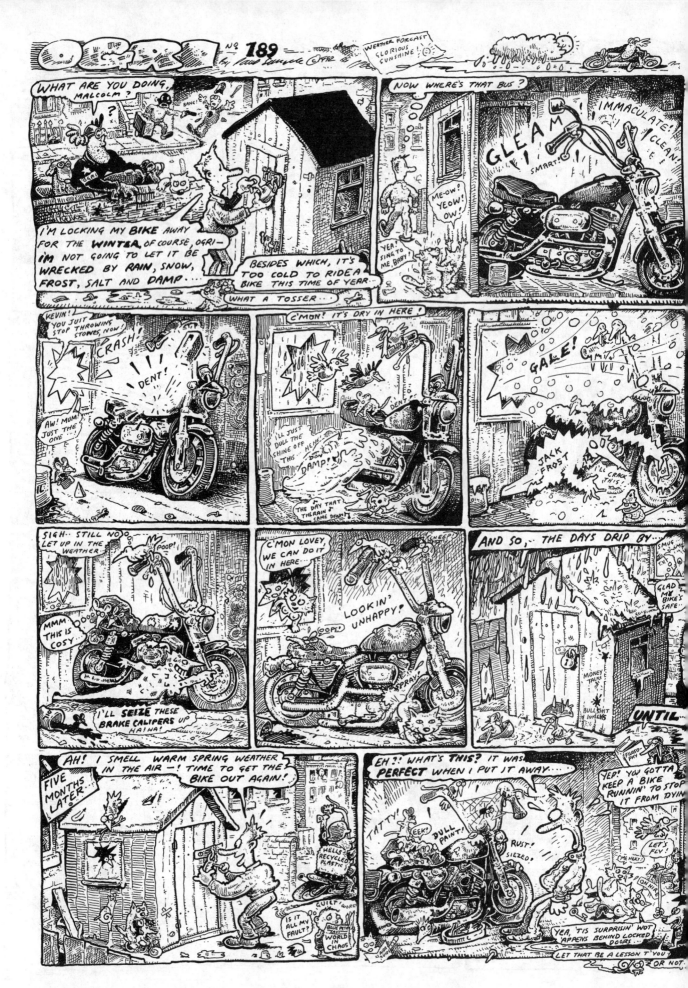

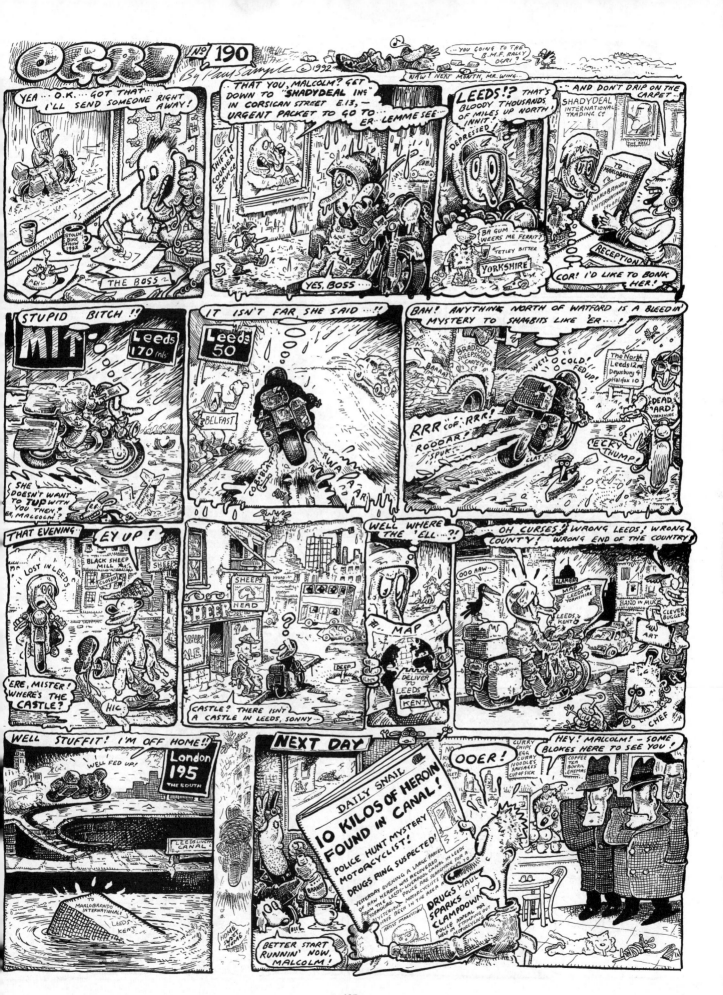

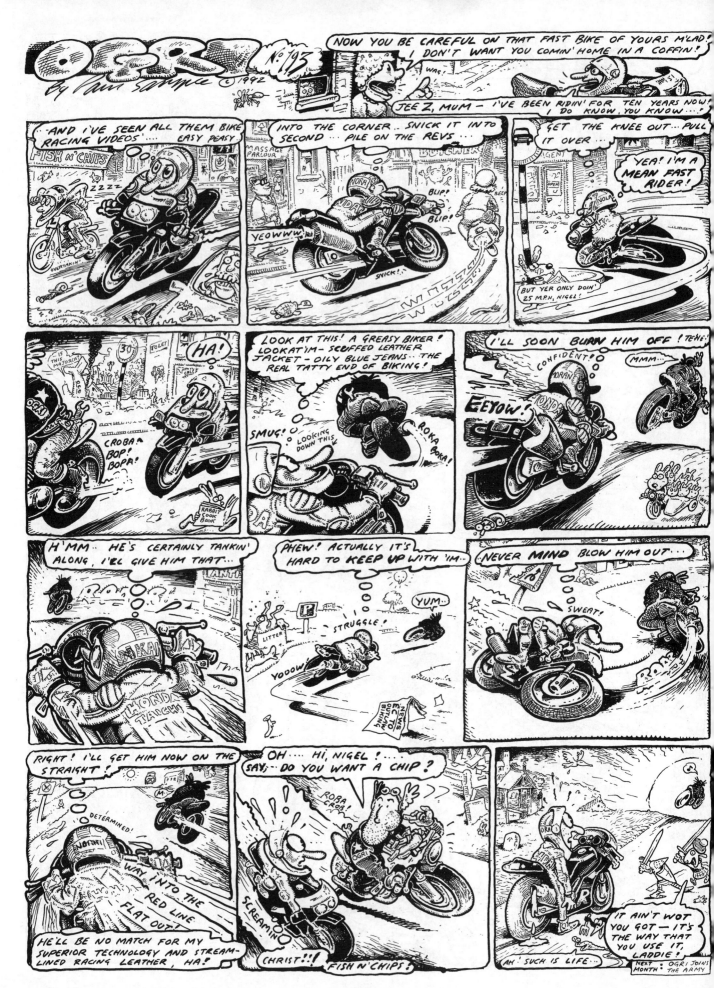